Your Place in the Son
Interactive Training Manual

A Guidebook for Groups

or Individuals

to

Discover and Experience

the Life that Jesus Died to Give You

Andy Hayner

ISBN: 1544106955
ISBN-13: 978-1544106953

DEDICATION

To Tina,
my wife and best friend,
Your walk with Jesus has impacted me more than you know.
Not only do I love you,
I admire you,
and all the more
even after all these years.

Thank you for walking this path with me.
Even now, I rejoice to think of
how great is your reward!

TABLE OF CONTENTS

INTRODUCTION

This interactive training manual is intended to provide a tool for ordinary believers to discover and walk in the supernatural life of Jesus Christ and impact the world around them. Although this training manual is based on my book, *Your Place in the Son,* it covers this material in an interactive fashion and can be used independently from the original book, making it perfect for small groups, discipleship relationships, and personal study.

This interactive training manual can be used in individually. However, it is designed especially for personal discipleship relationships and/or small groups to lay a solid foundation for a supernatural lifestyle of advancing the Kingdom of God. Although it can be used independently, group leaders are strongly encouraged to get the *Your Place in the Son* book, which provides more detailed examples important background information that will help you be fully prepared for questions you may face for yourself or others in your group.

Each chapter in this workbook is loaded with Biblical content and practical exercises, so it may be necessary to give yourselves more than one week to truly incorporate the teachings into your life. Each new lesson will activate you to walk in another aspect of living as a supernatural disciple of Jesus Christ.

Each lesson has a simple structure that facilitates personal interaction, Biblical learning, and hands-on activation. The usefulness and adaptability of this structure has been proven in the trenches of church planting movements around the world and in my own personal ministry as well.

Each lesson is divided into three sections 1) Look Back, 2) Lesson, and 3) Look Out.

The "Look Back" section gives everyone an opportunity to share highlights from the past week in two specific areas. People are encouraged to share any insights, lessons, or encouragement from what God is doing *in us* to change us more into the image of Jesus Christ. Also, everyone is asked to share a highlight from something that God has done *through us to touch others*. This keeps the focus on God (instead of ourselves) and facilitates the body of Christ connecting in a meaningful way as we pass on to others what Jesus Christ has given to us.

The "Lesson" section of the meeting is spent looking into the Word of God together. The Scripture is our teacher and the Holy Spirit is our guide as we directly interact with the Scriptures together. Every lesson is packed with Scriptures and guiding questions with specific points of observation to help you draw out life changing revelations. Together, you will have your eyes opened to the treasures of God's Word as the Spirit of God works in His people so that we are fully trained and useful for every good work.

The "Look Out" section focuses implementing the truths we have discovered *outside of our meeting time*. Each "Look Out" portion of the meeting has a time to practice, plan, and pray. You will do things like role play exercises, hands-on ministry, make plans for various personal or ministry objectives, and (of course) pray for one another.

We are called to make disciples of Jesus Christ, not merely be disciples ourselves. Yet God's plan is to so transform our lives that others can clearly see Jesus Christ living through us, so that we can say, "Follow me as I follow Christ." As you follow Jesus, be sure to take other people with you. *I would encourage and challenge everyone who is going through this material to identify at least one other person that they can take through these same lessons.* This book provides a simple tool that anyone can use to make disciples. Not only will this benefit them, it will also benefit you. The best way to learn is to teach others!

By all means, resist the comfort zone of merely becoming a Bible study. Purpose to live it out! Live out your call as an children of Jesus Christ and impact the world around you!

Lastly, if you are leading a group that is going through this material, be sure to read Appendix 1- Suggestions for *Your Place in the Son* group leaders! Be sure to take advantage of the additional resources I have available at my website, FullSpeedImpact.com. You'll find lots of free online video messages and other equipping resources that will help you walk in the fullness of Jesus Christ and make disciples who do the same.

CHAPTER 1
THE COST OF ADOPTION

I. LOOK BACK-

How have you experienced **God at work *in you*** or **through you to touch others** this past week? Share a highlight or an insight that has encouraged you recently.

II. LESSON

Before you can truly live like a child of God, you must discover the fullness of the relationship with God that Jesus purchased for you. You must clearly see the heart of God towards you and receive the depths of the amazing privileges that are yours through Christ.

SECTION 1- RESCUED AND RESTORED

Jesus Christ is the key to entering into a full relationship with God.

As you read the following Scriptures:

a. UNDERLINE words and phrases that describe people apart from Jesus Christ

b. CIRCLE the words and phrases that show how Jesus makes a difference for us.

c. ANSWER any questions.

For while we were still weak, at the right time Christ died for the ungodly...but God shows his love for us in that while we were still sinners, Christ died for us...For if while we were enemies (of God) we were reconciled to God by the death of his Son, much more, now that we are reconciled, shall we be saved by his life. Rom 5:6,8,10

"and you were dead in the trespasses and sins in which you once walked, following the course of this world, following the prince of the power of the air, the spirit that is now at work in the sons of disobedience—among whom we all once lived in the passions of our flesh, carrying out the desires of the body and the mind, and were by nature children of wrath, like the rest of mankind. But God, being rich in mercy, because of the great love

with which he loved us, even when we were dead in our trespasses, made us alive together with Christ—by grace you have been saved" (Eph 2:1-5)

Summarize: In the previous verses, review the words you have underlined and make a list of the way people are described apart from Christ. People apart from Christ are…:

When people are at our worst, what did God do that demonstrates the value He places upon us? Why is that important to realize?

You can tell how much something is worth by how much someone is willing to pay for it. On your worst day, what was God willing to pay for you? What does that say about your value to God?

If God values every person enough to die for them, how should that impact the way we see ourselves and treat others?

"I will not leave you as orphans; I will come to you." Joh 14:18

From what you know, how does the mindset and lifestyle of an orphan differ from a child raised in a secure and loving home? Make a list below:

ORPHAN   LOVING HOME

REFLECTION:
In what ways do people act and think like spiritual orphans?

Why did Jesus never live like a spiritual orphan?

According to the verse above, how does Jesus save us from being spiritual orphans?

Because of Jesus you are no longer an orphan, on probation as a candidate for potential rejection and abandonment. Nor are you a slave who is required to maintain your place in God's house only by your work. No! God has made a way to adopt you as a son of God[1]. Through faith in Jesus, you can receive *the same relationship with God as Jesus Christ by God's grace*. When you begin to see what this means, everything changes.

We need to adjust the way we speak and think so that we can saturate ourselves in the truth that sets us free. Let's declare these truths out loud. As you do, put your heart into it. Be bold. Be strong.

DECLARE: "I believe in Jesus Christ. I am redeemed. I am forgiven. I am a brand new creation in Christ. The old is gone. I am no longer what I once was apart from Christ. I was powerless. I was ungodly. I was an enemy of God. I was under the domain of darkness and evil. I lived according to the flesh and the desires of my fleshly mind. Before I cared anything about God or doing His will, while I was an enemy of God, God demonstrated His love for me by dying for me. My worth to God is not determined by my behavior. My worth is established by the price He paid for me. I am worth the blood of Jesus Christ to God. I will not sell myself short and live like a slave of sin. I will live in the love of God. I will embrace my value to God and love my neighbor as myself. I will not judge people according to their behavior. I will value people according to the cross of Christ. I am loved by God. I am filled with God's love. God's love overflows from my life to each and every person."

---

[1] The Biblical term "sons" is used for all believers regardless of gender. I follow this convention. "Son" is gender inclusive term indicating that all believers, male or female, are adopted by God by partaking of the same relationship as THE Son.

SECTION 2- MORE THAN GETTING OUT OF HELL

The good news of God's forgiveness through the death and resurrection of Jesus Christ is usually presented in terms of God's desire to get us out of hell and into heaven. While this is certainly true, it's only partially true and in some ways misses the main point altogether. Is God nothing more than a heavenly airline ticket clerk, switching our destination point on our "eternal plane ticket"? God is doing so much more. In fact, in some ways, the gospel isn't so much about getting us into heaven after we die as much as it is about getting *heaven into us now* (and forever). God so wants to fill us that others could see Him in us. The gospel is about a Father with a passion to do what Fathers do— give life and love to children who bear His image and to raise them up to become everything they ever dreamed by the grace He imparts into them.

As you read the following Scriptures:
a. UNDERLINE words and phrases that indicate the kind of RELATIONSHIP Jesus died to give us.

b. CIRCLE the words and phrases that indicate WHAT GOD DID to make this relationship possible.

c. ANSWER any questions.

Blessed be the God and Father of our Lord Jesus Christ, who has blessed us in Christ with every spiritual blessing in the heavenly places, even as He chose us in him before the foundation of the world, that we should be holy and blameless before him. In love He predestined us for adoption as sons through Jesus Christ, according to the purpose of his will (Eph 1:3-5)

For those whom He (God) foreknew he also predestined to be conformed to the image of His Son, in order that He (Jesus Christ) might be the firstborn among many brothers. (Rom 8:29)

For Christ also suffered once for sins, the righteous for the unrighteous, that he might bring us to God, being put to death in the flesh but made alive in the spirit, 1Pe 3:18

According to the preceding verse, what brings us to God?
   a) Really good worship music
   b) Our heart-felt praise
   c) Proving our devotion to God by acts of service
   d) The death of Jesus Christ on the cross for us

What happens when people fail to realize the truth of what brings us to God?

How does it change the way we relate to God and others when we embrace the significance of Jesus' death for us— that *God came to bring us to Himself?*

giving thanks to the Father, who has qualified you to share in the inheritance of the saints in light. He has delivered us from the domain of darkness and transferred us to the kingdom of his beloved Son, in whom we have redemption, the forgiveness of sins. (Col 1:12-14)

Based on the verse above, how do you get qualified to be a child of God?

Based on the verse above, does God ever allow evil to have any dominion over a child of God?

God has adopted us as children into His family at great cost to Himself. He is bringing us to heaven because He is bringing us to Himself, into His eternal embrace, to become part of His family to be His very own children. God didn't send Jesus to die just to get us into heaven after we die, but to give us direct access to His presence (which is in heaven) and to make His presence visible on earth by the Holy Spirit dwelling in us NOW and forever! God's heart is completely tied up in this endeavor.

SECTION 3- THE PRICE TO MAKE ADOPTION SECURE
When it comes to adoption, the law is either your greatest ally or your greatest enemy. Because of the cross of Christ, for those who believe in Him the "rights

of law" are on our side. When we look at the cross, we need to see the loving heart of the Father paying the terrible price to rescue us from the orphanage of this world and make us part of His family forever. The cross is where God manifested the depths of His love and the tremendous value He places on us. For adoption, love isn't enough. For love to thrive it must be secure. It's got to be legal and permanent. So through the cross, God paid the overwhelming price to ensure that His children could never be snatched from His hands.

As you read the following Scriptures:
a. UNDERLINE words and phrases that indicate the RELATIONSHIP that God has with us through Jesus Christ

b. CIRCLE the words and phrases that indicate ANYTHING WE MUST DO TO RESPOND to God's grace in Christ

c. ANSWER any questions.

My sheep hear my voice, and I know them, and they follow me. I give them eternal life, and they will never perish, and no one will snatch them out of my hand. My Father, who has given them to me, is greater than all, and no one is able to snatch them out of the Father's hand. I and the Father are one."
(John 10:27-29)

To as many who received Him, to them He gave **the right** *to be called children of God, even to those who believe in His name.* (John 1:12)

But when the fullness of time had come, God sent forth his Son, born of woman, born under the law, to redeem those who were under the law, so that we might receive adoption as sons. And because you are sons, God has sent the Spirit of his Son into our hearts, crying, "Abba! Father!" *(Gal 4:4-6)*

According to THIS verse, Jesus Christ died for us in order to:
   a) To rescue us from hell
   b) To get us into heaven after we die
   c) To get us to attend church regularly
   d) Adopt us as sons and give us the gift of the Holy Spirit NOW and forever.

REFLECTION:
Why is it significant to realize that Jesus Christ died to give us the right and power to walk like sons of God NOW, and not merely to alter our eternal destiny?

SECTION 4- BUT WHAT ABOUT...

Read the verses below and answer the question that follow.

WHAT ABOUT...If a child of God sins?
If we confess our sins, he is faithful and just to forgive us our sins and to cleanse us from all unrighteousness. If we say we have not sinned, we make him a liar, and his word is not in us. My little children, I am writing these things to you so that you may not sin. But if anyone does sin, we have an advocate with the Father, Jesus Christ the righteous. He is the propitiation for our sins, and not for ours only but also for the sins of the whole world. (1Jn 1:9-2:2)

Based on these verses, when a child of God sins, does God turn against us? Or does He remain for us, providing for us a perfect Advocate who applies His perfect righteousness to our account?

Some might ask, "What if I forget to confess something?"
Based on these verses, if we confess our sins (the ones we become aware of), how much unrighteousness are we cleansed of?

Does God make our salvation dependent upon our perfect memory and self-evaluation (so that we must discern and confess absolutely every sin to be forgiven), or on the grace of God through Jesus Christ?

Does God extend His grace as an encouragement 1) to carry on in sin, or 2) to overcome sin in order to carry on in fellowship with God through Jesus Christ?

WHAT ABOUT... If I am attacked by the devil, or people, or experience personal loss?

Who shall separate us from the love of Christ? Shall tribulation, or distress, or persecution, or famine, or nakedness, or danger, or sword? As it is written, "For your sake we are being killed all the day long; we are regarded as sheep to be slaughtered." No, in all these things we are more than conquerors through him who loved us. For I am sure that neither death nor life, nor angels nor rulers, nor things present nor things to come, nor powers, nor height nor depth, nor anything else in all creation, will be able to separate us from the love of God in Christ Jesus our Lord. (Rom 8:35-39)

Based on these verses, does the gospel promise us an easy, comfortable life? Or does the gospel promise us the love of God that empowers us to live in victory in any circumstance?

Why is this important to understand?

True or False:

_____ If you are going through difficulties, it's a sure sign that you've done something to make God upset.

Through the cross, God makes our place in His family legally permanent. Our biological ties to sin, guilt, and satan were all legally severed by the death of His own Son at the cross. The Son took our place to give His life as a ransom for ours. God has satisfied the just requirements of His own law through Jesus Christ, so that God can set sinners free and still achieve perfect justice. Jesus died in our place! Now satan has lost all legal claims on our lives. Through the cross, no one but God can claim us as children. By taking our place in the human race, in His blood Jesus Christ has "paid our legal fine" so that we can take His place in God's family— the place of a son[2].

---

[2] For the New Testament believer, you are adopted as a "son" whether you are male or female because in Christ there is "neither male, nor female." I follow this Biblical convention of using the terminology of "son" as gender inclusive.

DECLARE these truths together, "Nothing can separate me from the love of God. I am in Christ. No one can snatch me out of the Father's hand. Trials may come. God is with me. Nothing can separate me from His love. Jesus Christ lives in me. I am bigger than any trial or power of hell. His victory is mine, now and forever.

III. LOOK OUT:

PRACTICE

With a partner, practice responding to the following scenario:

One of your friends comes to you and says, "You seem to really be close to God, but I'm not even sure God can stand me. I blow it all the time." How can you use some of the truths of this lesson to respond to your friend and encourage them?

b. Switch roles and allow your partner to practice their own response.

PLAN

a. This week, saturate yourself with the truths in this lesson by using the verses in this lesson each day as part of a personal time alone with God. Praise and thank God for all that He's done for you. Allow these truths to sink into your heart as you declare them back to God.

b. If anyone needs healing or prayer, lay hands and minister to one another.

CHAPTER 2
THE OLD IS GONE

I. LOOK BACK

How have you experienced **God at work** *in you* or *through you to touch others* this past week? Especially, share any highlights from your assignment last week.

II. LESSON

Jesus Christ did **not** come to fix you. He came to make you brand new. He doesn't want to improve you. He replaces the old you with a brand new you . Our new life in Christ is not a "repair job" for our old life. It's a replacement and an upgrade. It's a more significant upgrade than replacing an old broken down bicycle with a Harley Davidson. We've gone from broken creatures to beings who have become partakers of the divine nature, recipients of the gift of eternal life. For us to live in the fullness of Jesus Christ, we must understand and truly see this reality.

SECTION 1- ORGANIC UNION, Foundations
(Take turns reading this section aloud and answering the questions together.)
One of the easiest ways to understand God's perspective on the finished work of the cross is to begin to see "organically", which means to understand how God sees the entire human race in terms of "organic union".

Here are a few examples that will help you to grasp the perspective of "organic union":

- When you hold an apple seed, you are not just holding an apple seed. You are holding an entire apple orchard. Why? Organic union. The "life of the apple" is in the seed. So the seed makes apple trees, which make apples which contain more seeds, which makes more trees, etc.

- If your grandfather had died before he met your grandmother, do you think you would be here?

- If Noah's ark had sunk to the bottom of the sea during the flood, would any of us be here?

The correct answer for the previous questions is "NO". The reason that the correct answer is "NO" is because of "organic union". Your life was INSIDE of your grandparents, and also inside of Noah (or his sons). So from God's perspective of "organic union" when God saved Noah, he was not only saving him and his family. He was saving the entire human race that was inside of Noah. This means that you and I were riding on Noah's ark. We are "organically" one life.

Select the best answer. If your father is taken captive, exiled, and enslaved, when you are born, you are:

a) Born in slavery to the same captors

b) Born with a lack of privileges and power

c) Born with a lack of resources

d) All of the above

Select the best answer. If your Father is a king and your mother is a queen, when you are born, you are:

a) Born royalty

b) Born with resources suited to your destiny

c) Born with privileges and power

d) All of the above

When your life is IN a slave, you are born in slavery. When your life is in a king, you are born royalty. We inherit the same position and powers.

This perspective is seen throughout the Bible, and culminates in the ultimate union—Jesus took on our human life so that we could receive His divine life.

SECTION 2- ORGANIC UNION, The Incarnation and the Cross

Thus it is written, "The first man Adam became a living being"; the last Adam (Jesus Christ) *became a **life-giving spirit**. (1Co 15:45)*
When God created Adam, the first man, the entire human race (including you and me) were inside of Adam. We were "organically" one. We shared one life, one nature, one destiny. When Adam yielded to sin, the entire human race was taken captive to sin too because we were inside of him.

1) In the following Scriptures,

a. UNDERLINE the phrases that indicate effects of our organic union with ADAM

Therefore, just as sin came into the world through one man, and death through sin, and so death spread to all men because all sinned... Therefore, as one trespass led to condemnation for all men... (Rom 5:12, 17)

And you were dead in the trespasses and sins in which you once walked, following the course of this world, following the prince of the power of the air, the spirit that is now at work in the sons of disobedience—among whom we all once lived in the passions of our flesh, carrying out the desires of the body and the mind, and were by nature children of wrath, like the rest of mankind. (Eph 2:1-3)

From the previous verses, summarize the results of being organically united to Adam:

Based on the truths above, how does this help us understand why God's plan is not merely to give us more teaching to help us aspire to "be better people"?

2) Read the Scriptures below. Answer the questions that follow.

He (Jesus Christ) *is the image of the invisible God, the firstborn of all creation. For by Him all things were created, in heaven and on earth, visible and invisible, whether thrones or dominions or rulers or authorities—all things were created through Him and for Him. And He is before all things, and in Him all things hold together. (Col 1:15-17)*

Select the best answer. According to these verses, when Jesus Christ came into the world, how old was Jesus?

   a) Less than one minute old. He was just a baby.

   b) Spiritually, this baby is the "Ancient of Days", the uncreated eternal God who IS before all things, older than time itself

   c) Both A and B

Select the best answer. According to the passage above, Jesus Christ:
   a) is the firstborn of all creation, holding the honor of the highest ranking being in all creation
   b) is the uncreated Creator of everything that is
   c) exists even now before and beyond all creation, outside of the bounds of time and space, holding together all of creation.
   d) Mind blown! All of the above!

In Jesus Christ, the creator God has joined the human race and stepped into His own creation. The moment that Jesus Christ was born, He immediately becomes the oldest human being to ever live…even older than Adam himself. Jesus Christ is the "firstborn of all creation." Although His human life was new, He was at the same time possessing a life that originated before and extends beyond time itself. He possessed *eternal life*. Consequently Jesus Christ became the new head of the human race. The whole human race was now INSIDE of Him (spiritually), just as the human race was inside of Adam (physically) at the beginning.

But when the fullness of time had come, God sent forth his Son, born of woman, born under the law, to redeem those who were under the law, so that we might receive adoption as sons. And because you are sons, God has sent the

Spirit of his Son into our hearts, crying, "Abba! Father!" So you are no longer a slave, but a son, and if a son, then an heir through God. (Gal 4:4-7)

Answer True or False based on the previous verses.

_____ Before Jesus Christ was born of woman, He was already the Son of God.

_____ God's Son become "organically united to our humanity" by becoming human to redeem us by His death so that we could become born of God's Spirit.

The Eternal View of the Cross

God cannot die… *as God.* Yet, when God became man in Jesus Christ, He was able to live and die as a man. But because He is also the head of the human race, when He died, the entire race of humanity that is inside of Him died in His death. Just like Noah's ship, *Jesus Christ contained the entire old humanity.* In His life, Jesus fulfilled all righteousness. In His redeeming death, God wrote "it is finished" over the entire old creation. This is God's perspective.

In the following Scriptures,

a. UNDERLINE the phrases that indicate God's perspective of WHO died when Christ died on the cross.

I have been crucified with Christ. It is no longer I who live, but Christ who lives in me. And the life I now live in the flesh I live by faith in the Son of God, who loved me and gave himself for me. (Gal 2:20)

For you have died, and your life is hidden with Christ in God. (Col 3:3)

We know that our old self was crucified with him in order that the body of sin might be brought to nothing (Rom. 6:6)

For the love of Christ controls us, because we have concluded this: that one has died for all, therefore all have died; and he died for all, that those who live might no longer live for themselves but for him who for their sake died and was raised. (2Co 5:14-15)

Why does it allow the love of Christ to control you once you conclude that everyone (including yourself) has already died in Christ?

But far be it from me to boast except in the cross of our Lord Jesus Christ, by which the world has been crucified to me, and I to the world. (Gal 6:14)

Because the entire human race was crucified in Christ, how should this impact our current relationship with everything in this present world?

Visual Summary
Stage 1- Adam falls under the power of sin… with us inside Him.

Stage 2- Jesus Christ becomes the Last Adam and dies on the Cross… with us inside of Him.

Stage 3- Jesus Christ rose from the dead with our "new creation life" *inside of Him* **for all who repent and believe to escape the nature and fate of Adam's corrupt race.**

The old is gone.   The New has come.

Therefore, if anyone is in Christ, he is a new creation. The old has passed away; behold, the new has come. (2Co 5:17)

In this the love of God was made manifest among us, that God sent his only Son into the world, so that we might live through him. (1Jn 4:9)

In the following Scriptures

a) Underline: Anything we must do in order to experience life in Christ

b) Circle: What happens to those who remain united to Adam and do not receive life in Christ.

Whoever believes in the Son has eternal life; whoever does not obey the Son shall not see life, but the wrath of God remains on him. (John 3:36)

Whoever does not honor the Son does not honor the Father who sent him. Truly, truly, I say to you, whoever hears my word and believes him who sent me has eternal life. He does not come into judgment, but has passed from death to life. (John 5:23-24)

because, if you confess with your mouth that Jesus is Lord and believe in your heart that God raised him from the dead, you will be saved. For with the heart one believes and is justified, and with the mouth one confesses and is saved. (Rom 10:9-10)

We know that our old self was crucified with him in order that the body of sin might be brought to nothing, so that we would no longer be enslaved to sin. For the death he (Jesus Christ) died he died to sin, once for all, but the life he lives he lives to God. So you also must consider yourselves dead to sin and alive to God in Christ Jesus. Let not sin therefore reign in your mortal body, to make you obey its passions. Do not present your members to sin as instruments for unrighteousness, but present yourselves to God as those who have been brought from death to life, and your members to God as instruments for righteousness. (Rom 6:6,10-13)

In the following Scriptures,

a. Circle the phrases that indicate the reality and effects of our organic union with JESUS CHRIST.

For if, because of one man's trespass, death reigned through that one man, much more will those who receive the abundance of grace and the free gift of righteousness reign in life through the one man Jesus Christ. Therefore, as one trespass led to condemnation for all men, so one act of righteousness leads to justification and life for all men. For as by the one man's disobedience the many were made sinners, so by the one man's obedience the many will be made righteous. (Rom 5:16-20)

Select the best answer. According to the Scripture, believer's righteousness is based on:
   a) **our own obedience**
   b) **the obedience of Jesus Christ and our faith in Him**

Remember that you were at that time separated from Christ, alienated from the commonwealth of Israel and strangers to the covenants of promise, having no hope and without God in the world. But now in Christ Jesus you who once were far off have been brought near by the blood of Christ. (Eph 2:12-13)

Based on the <u>two previous Scripture passages</u>, use the chart below to categorize the words that are associated with life "in Adam" vs. "in Christ".

<u>Old Creation versus New Creation Realities</u>

IN ADAM	IN CHRIST

Therefore, if anyone is in Christ, he is a new creation. The old has passed away; behold, the new has come. (2Co 5:17)

We are going to make declarations using this chart. According to God's Word, everything on Adam's side is GONE, and only those things IN Christ remain.

Declare, in Jesus Name, _____ is GONE and has *no place in me*. In Christ, I AM _____.

MAIN POINT- Your entire life apart from Jesus Christ has already been crucified. You are now free to discover and walk in the new life we receive from Jesus Christ. Our new self is our only true self. God does not want us to merely "put on the new self" to cover over the "old self". We are to "put off the old self" as part of "putting on new self".

III.   LOOK OUT

PRACTICE

God's Word tells us to "**put off your old self,** *which belongs to your former manner of life and is corrupt through deceitful desires, and to be renewed in the spirit of your minds, and to* **put on the new self, created after the likeness of God in true righteousness and holiness.**"(Eph 4:22-24)

Discussion: How does the reality of our organic union with Jesus Christ rescue us from approaching the Christian life as merely "self-improvement program with the Bible as a reference guide"?

Partner up for Role play. Using the truths in this lesson, take role playing and responding to the following scenarios:

    A. You are out with a friend that you are confident really knows the Lord. You asked them how things are going in their walk with God. They open up to you and share, "Honestly, I'm really struggling right now under a pile of guilt. I don't normally do this, but for some reason, curiosity I guess, I ended up getting sucked into a porno site. I know I'm forgiven, but I just feel so yukky. It's really hard for me to pray right now. I don't even know why I'm telling you this."

- Begin to respond to your friend by explaining the difference between our "old self" and "new self".

- Change roles. After hearing your explanation, your friend asks, "Practically HOW we can "put off the old" and "put on the new". I don't want to go back. Share with your friend in practical terms, how to put off the old and put on the new.

PLAN

Jesus Christ took on flesh to become one with your "flesh life". In His death, your life apart from Him has been crucified. The source of all your struggles, downfalls, fears, shame, guilt, and brokenness has all been crucified. Jesus Christ sets us free from ourselves.

This week, purpose to focus on this aspect of the gospel by spending time each day praising God, thanking God, and declaring your freedom from your "old man" and all its ways.

CHAPTER 3
WELCOME TO YOUR PLACE IN THE SON
PART 1

I. LOOK BACK-
How have you experienced *God at work in you* as you declared your freedom from the "old you apart from Christ" in your daily, personal times alone with God?

II. LESSON
Children tend to express what they receive from their fathers. Hurt, broken fathers tend to raise hurt, broken children that often grow up to be hurt, broken people. Secure, loving fathers tend to raise secure, loving children.

No matter what sort of relationship you may have experienced with your earthly father, *Jesus has come to give you **His relationship with His Heavenly Father as a gift.*** You can experience this reality through the Holy Spirit.

SECTION 1- The Father's Relationship with His Son
The Christian life isn't merely adopting a change of behavior and values. It's entering into a new relationship with God that ushers you into a whole new lifestyle— the very same relationship with God that Jesus had.

From before the world began, the Father's one great passion is to pour Himself with all His love into His Son by the Holy Spirit. His greatest thrill is the Son's pleasure in His love. The Son's primary activity receiving all the perfections of His Father's fullness by the Spirit and putting them on display in glory. *You were created to participate in this relationship!*

When Jesus came, He came to put His Father on display by making His eternal relationship with the Father visible to all. Then He paid the price *for us to receive **His relationship with the Father** as our very own.*

As you read the following Scriptures:

a. UNDERLINE words and phrases that show the kind of RELATIONSHIP THAT THE FATHER AND SON enjoy with one another.

b. CIRCLE the words and phrases that show the LIFESTYLE/BEHAVIOR that the Son's relationship with the Father produced in the Son.

c. ANSWER any questions.

And when Jesus was baptized, immediately he went up from the water, and behold, the heavens were opened to him, and he saw the Spirit of God descending like a dove and coming to rest on him; and behold, a voice from heaven said, "This is my beloved Son, with whom I am well pleased."..."Behold, my servant whom I have chosen, my beloved with whom my soul is well pleased. I will put my Spirit upon him, and he will proclaim justice to the Gentiles." ..."He was still speaking when, behold, a bright cloud overshadowed them, and a voice from the cloud said, "This is my beloved Son, with whom I am well pleased; listen to him." (Mat 3:16-17, 12:18, 17:5)

How do you think it must feel to hear God speaking from eternity, "You are my beloved. I've chosen you. I support you. I take great pleasure in you. I give you My Spirit, my power and presence?" What difference would that make in your life?

Col. 3:12 says, "*Put on then, <u>as God's chosen ones, holy and beloved,</u> compassionate hearts, kindness, humility, meekness, and patience.*" (Col 3:12)

How much of what the Father says about Jesus Christ does He say about each one of us who believes in Jesus Christ?

What kind of character will taking this to heart produce in us?

According to these verses, what is the kind of lifestyle that is consistent with a true spiritual confidence of God's love?

Personalize these truths. Declare aloud what the Father speaks over you. Allow your heart to listen to the Father's heart. "You are in Christ. I have adopted you as My son. I have chosen you. You are my Beloved, one with my Son. I have given you My Holy Spirit. I take great pleasure in You. You fulfill My purposes on the earth and I am setting the captives free through you."

Continue to read the verses below and Underline, Circle, and Answer questions according to the instructions previously given.

But Jesus answered them, "My Father is working until now, and I am working." This was why the Jews were seeking all the more to kill him, because not only was he breaking the Sabbath, but he was even calling God his own Father, making himself equal with God. So Jesus said to them, "Truly, truly, I say to you, the Son can do nothing of his own accord, but only what he sees the Father doing. For whatever the Father does, that the Son does likewise. For the Father loves the Son and shows him all that he himself is doing. And greater works than these will he show him, so that you may marvel. (John 5:17-20)

Some people's mindsets towards God are driven by fear of rejection and punishment. As a result, they are afraid that if they truly embrace being loved and accepted as a son of God, they would begin to live a life of sin. However, Jesus was very aware that the Father "loves the Son". How did this awareness of the Father's love impact Jesus' lifestyle?

What does this show about how receiving the Father's love will impact our lifestyle?

The words that I say to you I do not speak on my own authority, but the Father who dwells in me does his works. Believe me that I am in the Father and the Father is in me, or else believe on account of the works themselves. (John14:10-11)

So Jesus said to them, "When you have lifted up the Son of Man, then you will know that I am he, and that I do nothing on my own authority, but speak just as the Father taught me. And he who sent me is with me. He has not left me alone, for I always do the things that are pleasing to him." (John 8:28-29)

In what way does Jesus' description of His relationship with His Father in the verses above overlap with His words to us *"All authority in heaven and on earth has been given to me. Go therefore and make disciples of all nations… And behold, I am with you always, to the end of the age?" (Mat 28:18-20)*

Whose authority did Jesus express? Whose authority should we express?

Who sent Jesus? Who sent us?

Was Jesus alone? Are we left alone?

What's the relationship between Jesus' presence with us and carrying out His mission in this world?

And this is eternal life, that they know you the only true God, and Jesus Christ whom you have sent. I glorified you on earth, having accomplished the work that you gave me to do. And now, Father, glorify me in your own presence with the glory that I had with you before the world existed. "I have manifested your name to the people whom you gave me out of the world (John 17:3-5)

How does Jesus define eternal life- quantity of time? Or quantity of revelation and relationship?

How does Jesus' definition of eternal life point us to how we can experience our life in eternity NOW?

For as the Father has life in himself, so he has granted the Son also to have life in himself. (John 5:26)

Evil works in our lives by tricking us to try and find life for our souls in something of this world (e.g. possessions, relationships, fame, etc.). How did it make a difference for Jesus, that *the Father* had given Him divine, eternal "life *in Himself*"?

REFLECTION

Have you ever experienced something like "life for your soul" from a personal relationship or an activity or an achievement?

How have you experienced "life in yourself" from your relationship with God?

III. LOOK OUT
PRACTICE

The foundation of our relationship with God is the revelation that God has given us in His Word. By using the Word of God as the basis of fellowshipping with God, we can encounter God personally. There are many ways in which we can do this. For this exercise, we will use Psalm 23, but you can use any Scripture that is giving any direct revelation of God's character or works.

A. **Worshipping, praising, and thanking God personally, from the heart.**

Perhaps the simplest, and most natural way to fellowship with God by using the Word is to proceed slowly through a passage that speaks directly of His character, nature and works, phrase by phrase, and then to personally express your love, worship, praise and thanks to God from your heart as a response.

For example, read "*The LORD is my shepherd; I shall not want…*"

You can respond back to God in love and adoration… "God, you are the Lord over all things. I love you Lord. You watch over me, like a shepherd.

You protect me. Thank you for your protection. I am safe in your care, etc…" Just allow your heart to soar with faith, love, and truth.

After you've touched the heart of God and allowed God's heart to touch yours, move on to read and respond to the next phrase. This creates a powerful interaction, a dialogue with God, that can be truly life changing.

As a group complete the remainder of Psalm 23. Take turns reading a phrase, then responding with personal expressions of praise, trust, and thanks.

He makes me lie down in green pastures. He leads me beside still waters. He restores my soul.

He leads me in paths of righteousness for his name's sake.

Even though I walk through the valley of the shadow of death, I will fear no evil, for you are with me; your rod and your staff, they comfort me. You prepare a table before me in the presence of my enemies;

You anoint my head with oil; my cup overflows. Surely goodness and mercy shall follow me all the days of my life,

and I shall dwell in the house of the LORD forever.

B. Beholding the Father and the Son

Another powerful way that we can encounter God is by learning to "behold the Father and the Son." We do this by faith, using the Scriptures, purposing to see how Jesus, "the Word made flesh", may express the truths contained in Scripture directly to the Father… and vice versa.

For example, we can take Psalm 23, that begins, "The Lord is my shepherd…" and ask, "How might Jesus personally express this to His Father while living on earth?" After all, the same Spirit that expressed love and faith through the one who wrote Psalm 23 is the very Spirit that lived in Jesus Christ. Isn't Jesu Christ called, "The Lamb of God?" Then He must need a Shephard. So we can also ask how might the Father express Himself to His Son as the Shephard? As you express this by faith, you can actually behold the Father and the Son by the Spirit in a very powerful way.

> *"Father, the Son is your perfect Lamb. You are His perfect Shepherd. You care for Him. He depends completely upon You. He is safe in your care, so secure. He loves your leadership. You love to lead Him and watch over Him. Jesus, you are the perfect Lamb of God. You are unafraid. You trust in His care. You look to Him for everything, and your soul is in perfect peace."*

As you allow your heart to enter in, with love and gratitude, you will experience the transforming power of this way of using the Scriptures to behold the Father and Son. *In beholding the relationship between the Father and the Son, you are beholding the relationship that you have received in Christ.*

Tips:
- Use your own words. Keep it simple. Don't over think it.
- This is a powerful form of Scripture meditation and intimate communion with God.
- Find the truth in the Scripture, then trace that truth back into the heart of the Father and the Son.
- Consider point of view of both the Son and the Father as they would express themselves to one another in undying, eternal fellowship.
- This is a great way to get your eyes off yourself, because you are not directly involved, except as an observer.

For this exercise, taking turns, go phrase by phrase using the remainder of Psalm 23 to behold the Father and the Son expressing their love and trust to one another in the truths of these Scriptures.

PLAN
This week, use these two approaches to fellowshipping with God in the Scriptures, using Psalm 23 several times through the remainder of the week. As you do, allow your heart to enter in by faith. At the end of the week, take note of the effect that fellowshipping with God like this has on your own soul.

CHAPTER 4
WELCOME TO YOUR PLACE IN THE SON
PART 2

I. LOOK BACK-

How have you experienced God at work in you as you beheld the Son and the Father using Psalm 23 that we covered last week in your daily, personal times alone with God?

II. LESSON
SECTION 1-UNDERSTANDING YOUR SPIRIT

In order to grasp your union with Jesus Christ, you must understand the unique features of your spirit, your soul, and your body.

In the Scriptures below,
a. UNDERLINE the phrases that refer to YOUR SPIRIT or YOUR UNION with Christ in the spirit
b. CIRCLE the phrases that refer to YOUR SOUL (your mind, emotions/desires, and will)
c. DRAW A BOX AROUND the phrases that refer to YOUR BODY
d. ANSWER any questions based on the verses directly preceding the question.

Now may the God of peace himself sanctify you completely, and may your whole spirit and soul and body be kept blameless at the coming of our Lord Jesus Christ. 1 Thes.5:23

In that day (when the Holy Spirit is sent) *you will know that I* (Jesus) *am in my Father, and you in me, and I in you. Whoever has my commandments and keeps them, he it is who loves me. And he who loves me will be loved by my Father, and I will love him and manifest myself to him." (John 14:20,21)*

If you are inside the glorified Jesus Christ in the presence of the Father, how do you look to the Father?

If Jesus is in the Father and inside of you, how close are you to God?

Is it possible to know these things *by experience* instead of just "theory"? If so, how (according to these verses)?

But he who is joined to the Lord is one spirit with Him. (1Co 6:17)

If it was the Spirit of Jesus Christ that made Him amazing, what does that mean for you?

For by a single offering He has perfected for all time those who are being sanctified. (Heb 10:14)

According to this verse, what did the offering of Jesus Christ do to you? For how long?

Based on the verse above, complete this sentence:

Because of the blood of Jesus Christ, I am_____

even while my life is being set apart for God.

Now SAY IT! (God does!)

SECTION 2- STEPPING INTO THE "SON'S PLACE"

What if **you** could have *Jesus' relationship with Jesus' Father*? How different would your life be? The good news is that, through Jesus Christ, God has given us the same relationship with Him as he has with Jesus Christ. We get to "put on Christ" before the Father and live with God as a son inside THE Son.

In each of the Scriptures for this section

a. UNDERLINE Any words or phrases that indicate that God has given us the RELATIONSHIP that He has with Jesus Christ as our relationship, for us to enjoy

b. CIRCLE those phrases that indicate *HOW WE CAN PARTAKE* of the Son's relationship with the Father as our own experience

c. ANSWER any questions.

God is faithful, by whom you were called into the fellowship of his Son, Jesus Christ our Lord. 1 Cor. 1:9

When you think about the kind of fellowship the Father has with His Son, what are some words or phrases that you would use to describe that fellowship?

Why is it important for your daily life to realize that God has called YOU into "the fellowship of His Son"?

How is being called by God to enter into the fellowship He shares with His Son better/different than merely being invited to establish your own relationship with God?

Jesus said, "I am the door. If anyone enters through Me, He will be saved and will go in and out and find pasture." John 10:9

What does Jesus' metaphor mean by going beyond merely "being saved" to an ongoing experience with God "entering through Jesus" to "go in" and "find pasture"? How is experiencing God's presence through Jesus Christ like a sheep going into a field to "find pasture"?

How do we "go in" to nourish our souls in fellowship with God *through Him*?

"I will not leave you as orphans; I will come to you. Yet a little while and the world will see me no more, but you will see me. Because I live, you also will live. In that day (when Jesus sends the Holy Spirit) you will know that I am in my Father, and you in me, and I in you. (John 14:18-20)

Does Jesus believe we can actually EXPERIENCE the fact that Jesus lives in His Father, and we live inside of Him, and He lives inside of us?

What makes this experience possible?
How are you actively cooperating with the Holy Spirit to make these things that

Jesus speaks about your own personal experience?

May grace and peace be multiplied to you in the knowledge of God and of Jesus our Lord. His divine power has granted to us all things that pertain to life and godliness, through the knowledge of him who called us to his own glory and excellence, by which he has granted to us his precious and very great promises, so that through them you may become partakers of the divine nature, having escaped from the corruption that is in the world because of sinful desire. (2Pe 1:2-4)
If God has "granted to us all things", how much is He willing to allow us to become "partakers" of?

What difference does that make?

Jesus says, *"Abide in me, and I in you. As the branch cannot bear fruit by itself, unless it abides in the vine, neither can you, unless you abide in me. I am the vine; you are the branches. Whoever abides in me and I in him, he it is that bears much fruit, for apart from me you can do nothing. John 15:4-5*

(Abide is related to the word, "abode" and means to dwell or live in, to make it your home. Jesus wants us to live inside of Him as our permanent residence.)

Select the best answer. What is the key to experiencing Jesus living through us to impact the world around us?
    a) a Bible college degree
    b) fasting, sacrifice, discipline and a five year plan
    c) getting a spiritual impartation from a powerful man of God
    d) dwelling in spiritual union with Jesus Christ and allowing Him to live inside of you

Therefore, since we have been justified by faith, we have peace with God through our Lord Jesus Christ. Through him we have also obtained access by faith into this grace in which we stand, and we rejoice in hope of the glory of God. Rom. 5:1-2

> Justified means more than "just forgiven" or "just as if I never sinned". It is not only that our sin-debt has been paid so that we are back to a zero balance. Justified means that we are counted to be completely righteous, as if we have done everything God every wanted. How cool is that?!!!

What would change in the way you relate to God if you truly see yourself this way?

According to this verse, does discovering that Jesus Christ made us right with God apart from our own works set us free to a) sin without worry, or b) to enter into God's presence and be transformed into the likeness of His glory? Why is this important to grasp?

So you also must consider yourselves dead to sin and alive to God in Christ Jesus...Do not present your members to sin as instruments for unrighteousness, but present yourselves to God as those who have been brought from death to life, and your members to God as instruments for righteousness. Rom. 6:11-13

What is the difference between merely presenting yourself to God, and presenting yourself to God as those who are alive from the dead, seated with Christ in heavenly places?

Based on this, how does the gospel change how you should "consider yourself" and how you speak about yourself, and how you "present yourself"?

REFLECTION

Many people are very negative about themselves. Based on what you've learned in this lesson, does the way in which you think and speak about yourself need to change, so that it matches what God says about you? If so, in what ways?

III. LOOK OUT

PRACTICE

1. **Declarations**- Each person should select one or more of the verses in the section "Stepping into the Son's Place" from this lesson, to turn them into prayer and declarations of faith. Taking turns leading declarations, the others will repeat what the leader says. Use the Scriptures as a launching pad and let your heart soar into the embrace of the Father!

For example, John 10:9-Jesus said, *"I am the door. If anyone enters by me, he will be saved and will go in and out and find pasture."*

Leader: Jesus, you are the door (group repeats) I have entered into you (group repeats) Everything I am outside of you is gone (group repeats) I step into you into the Father's presence. (group repeats) I am inside of Jesus Christ and I am saved (group repeats) I am wearing His righteousness (group repeats) He wore my sins (group repeats) I am inside of Jesus Christ and He is inside of Me (group repeats) I find nourishment for my soul in the Father's presence (group repeats).

Now each one pick a different verse from this lesson and take turns leading out in declarations of faith based on the verse you select until each one has taken a turn.

2) Role Play-

A. With a partner, practice responding to the following scenario:

You have friend who is a sincere believer in Jesus Christ. However, they have been raised in a very strict, often legalistic church environment. They struggle with a constant fear of rejection and feelings like God is never satisfied with them. They ask you over for coffee to seek your encouragement.

- How can you use your understanding of our union with God in Christ to help them begin to enjoy fellowship with God? You have five minutes.

- Switch roles and allow your partner to practice their own response.

B. With a partner, practice responding to the following scenario:

You have friend who has always lived on the wild side. You have lunch with them and share a little bit about the difference that Jesus Christ has been making in your life. They push back, "Well, I'm not really into religious stuff. No offense, but to me it seems like a bunch of rules and traditions that really don't fit my lifestyle." How can you use some of what you've been learning in this book to respond to him an help him to see that there is more?

PLAN

A. Every day for the next week (and the rest of your life), set aside some time speak to God from "inside of Jesus Christ". Enjoy the relationship that Father has with Jesus Christ as YOUR relationship. Dedicate this time *without speaking to God about any of your needs, failures, or things you need His help.* Simply be with God and enjoy the Father's relationship with the Son as your relationship. Spend enough time to allow your soul to "absorb" this perspective. Use the Scriptures in this chapter or others that are related to life in Christ as a spring board for these times. Ephesians 1, Romans 6, or Psalm 23 are easy places to start. [3]

---

[3] I have written *Spirit Cry- Declarations of a Child of God in the Embrace of the Father* as a devotional tool to help believers establish the practice of speaking and hearing from the Spirit of the Son of God in your heart by using God's Word. It is a unique and very powerful tool that can be very helpful to build this practice into your life.

B. Stop letting guilt, worry, and shame hold you back from the living in the Father's embrace. Stop chasing your satisfaction and security in the stuff you have and eyes of other people. Let the Love of God fill you. Let it control you!

CHAPTER 5
EMOTIONAL FREEDOM BY RENEWING YOUR MIND

I. LOOK BACK-
How have you experienced *God at work in you* and/or *God at work through you to impact people around* you this past week?

II. LESSON
Through faith in Jesus Christ, our spirits are made one with God, giving us direct access to His presence and power. However, we must learn to cooperate with the Spirit of God within us by being renewed in our soul (which is our mind, will, emotions). Through the power of the Spirit of God, we can experience inner freedom, joy, and peace. This is not automatic. Let's identify from the Scriptures principles that show us how to function in the power of the Spirit.

SECTION 1

Everyone has challenges in circumstances and relationships. Emotions aren't bad or wrong. However, when our emotions are driven by selfishness, lies, needs, and personal pain, we merely react "in the flesh". We must learn to let the Spirit of God and the truth of God's word govern our hearts.

In this section, we will identify some important truths regarding the relationship of our born-again spirit with our soul, which need to be governed by our spirit and the truth of God's Word.

Read the following Scriptures and answer the questions that follow based on the verses immediately preceding the questions.

My enemies trample on me all day long, for many attack me proudly. When I am afraid, I put my trust in you. In God, whose word I praise, in God I trust; I shall not be afraid. What can flesh do to me? (Psa 56:2-4)

Based on this Scripture, answer true or false for the following statements.

_____ **Experiencing fear is wrong. It's a sure sign of spiritual immaturity.**

_____ We should allow our faith to rule over our fear instead of allowing our fear to rule over our faith.

_____ If bad people do bad things to us, we have the right to react out of our fears or anger. After all, it's their fault for doing what they did to us.

_____ By the power of God's Spirit, we can walk in confident faith even when circumstances and people are nasty.

REFLECTION:
When have you felt threatened or personally insecure?

When people or circumstances are nasty, how do you tend to react if you respond out of your fears and insecurities?

What would change if you allowed confidence in God to govern your heart in those situations?

Why are you cast down, O my soul, and why are you in turmoil within me? Hope in God; for I shall again praise him, my salvation and my God. My soul is cast down within me; therefore I remember You (God). (Psa 42:5-6)

Based on this Scripture, answer true or false for the following statements.

_____ When our hearts feel hopeless, depressed, hurt, angry, and fearful, there's nothing we can do about it. That's just the way it is in this world.

_____ In order to move forward to emotional freedom, it's always necessary to analyze your feelings until you figure out why you feel the way you feel.

_____ God is "the God of hope." So, when our souls feel hopeless, it's because our hearts are listening more to our circumstances than to the gospel.

_____ It's NOT possible to stir up our spirit to function in faith, hope and love when our emotions are in turmoil.

_____ We can bring our emotions into agreement with God's Spirit by exercising faith and speaking God's truth to our troubled heart.

May the God of hope fill you with all joy and peace in believing, so that by the power of the Holy Spirit you may abound in hope. (Rom 15:13)

Based on <u>this Scripture</u>, answer true or false for the following statements.

_____ God can fill us with all joy and peace *whether we believe or not*. It's up to Him.

_____ We can only have joy, peace, and hope when our personal relationships and our circumstances line up to "God's perfect will".

_____ By faith in the gospel and the power of the Holy Spirit, we can be filled with joy and peace even in the midst of whatever troubles, trials, and attacks we may face in this world.

_____ If we are not filled with God's joy and peace, we should examine our beliefs— not merely our "doctrinal statements" but what we are functionally embracing as "truth" in our hearts.

SECTION 2- For each of the Scriptures for this section

a. UNDERLINE the phrases that indicate when we are operating in the FLESH/OLD MAN/or the UNRENEWED MIND

b. CIRCLE the phrases that indicate when we are operating in POWER OF THE HOLY SPIRIT.

c. DRAW A BOX AROUND words that indicate THINGS WE CAN DO PRACTICALLY to operate in the Spirit

d. ANSWER any questions based on the verses directly preceding the question.

Now the works of the flesh are evident: sexual immorality, impurity, sensuality, idolatry, sorcery, enmity, strife, jealousy, fits of anger, rivalries, dissensions, divisions, envy, drunkenness, orgies, and things like these. I warn you, as I warned you before, that those who do such things will not inherit the kingdom of God. But the fruit of the Spirit is love, joy, peace, patience, kindness, goodness, faithfulness, gentleness, self-control; against such things there is no law. And those who belong to Christ Jesus have crucified the flesh with its passions and desires. If we live by the Spirit, let us also keep in step with the Spirit. (Gal 5:19-25)

How is the way in which a tree bears fruit in nature similar to the way in which a believer exhibits the fruit of the Holy Spirit?

How would you describe the difference between merely having the Holy Spirit in us versus walking with the Holy Spirit step by step?

So now faith, hope, and love abide, these three; but the greatest of these is love. (1Co 13:13)

Choose the best answer.

We are functioning in the power of the Spirit of God when we are:
   a) Analyzing and trying to figure things out
   b) Reacting emotionally and trying to improve our mood
   c) Just doing what you are supposed to do
   d) Exercising FAITH, HOPE, and LOVE while taking our stand in union with Jesus Christ

For those who live according to the flesh set their minds on the things of the flesh, but those who live according to the Spirit set their minds on the things of the Spirit. For to set the mind on the flesh is death, but to set the mind on the Spirit is life and peace. For the mind that is set on the flesh is hostile to God, for it does not submit to God's law; indeed, it cannot. Those who are in the flesh cannot please God. You, however, are not in the flesh but in the Spirit, if in fact the Spirit of God dwells in you. (Rom 8:5-9)

Based on <u>this Scripture</u>, answer true or false for the following statements.

_____ When we are operating in the mind of the Spirit, the automatic result is that God's life (i.e. spiritual power) and peace are unleashed to operate in our souls.

_____ We experience the Spirit of God dwelling in our SOULS with His life and peace only to the degree that we operate by the mindset of the Holy Spirit.

_____ If we are experiencing "the touch of death" and/or a "lack of life and peace" it is because we have a "self-oriented/fleshly mindset" in that area.

Now this I say and testify in the Lord, that you must no longer walk as the Gentiles do, in the futility of their minds. They are darkened in their understanding, alienated from the life of God because of the ignorance that is in them, due to their hardness of heart. They have become callous and have given themselves up to sensuality, greedy to practice every kind of impurity. But that is not the way you learned Christ!—assuming that you have heard Him and were taught in Him, as the truth is in Jesus, to put off your old self, which belongs to your former manner of life and is corrupt through deceitful desires, and to be renewed in the spirit of your minds, and to put on the new self, created after the likeness of God in true righteousness and holiness. Therefore, having put away falsehood, let each one of you speak the truth with his neighbor, for we are members one of another. (Eph 4:17-25)

Based on this Scripture, select the best answer.
The gospel instructs believers to:
  a) Continually strive to improve yourself to prove your love and devotion to God.
  b) Put off their old self (because it has been put to death and can never be improved).
  c) Realize your new self is already like God, holy and righteous. Put on your new self.
  d) All of the above
  e) B & C, but NOT A

Because the Spirit of God dwells in us, believers can be renewed in the Spirit that operates in our minds by:

    a) Analyzing our past to understand ourselves better

    b) Hearing Jesus Christ directly

    c) Embracing the truth we hear from Jesus Christ and putting away lies

    d) All of the above

    e) B & C, but NOT A

III. LOOK OUT-
PRACTICE- KEYS to EMOTIONAL & MENTAL FREEDOM

Many people are trying to follow Christ carrying emotional baggage. It slows them down. Many people have been badly treated by others and still carry this pain around in their hearts. Most people have occasional feelings of inadequacy, worthlessness, shame, guilt, powerlessness, fear, or rejection. But take a look at those painful words—worthlessness, rejection, shame, guilt, powerlessness. These are not just feelings. These are feelings wrapped around **beliefs** that feel true.

When we allow circumstances and the actions/words of other people (instead of Jesus) to have authority over our emotions, we come under the power of those lies, painful lies that cripple our soul and destroy our lives. These lies may *feel very true*, but through the power of the Gospel, we can be free! Remember, the truth is NOT found in your experiences or your feelings. It's found in Jesus Christ, and HE dwells inside of you to set you free!

KEYS TO FREEDOM FOR SOULS: For the remainder of this lesson, we will learn a simple way to experience the freedom of Jesus Christ in our souls Let's break this down into a **simple 3 step process** that you can use:

1) Identify the lies in the pain.

2) Receive and practice the truth.

3) Forgive others, yourself, and God from the heart.

STEP BY STEP:

1. **Identify the lies in the pain:** You can identify the lie in the pain by completing the following question(s), "I feel <u>(fill in the blank)</u>? Why? <u>(answer)</u>" For example, "I feel worthless" The lie is "You are worthless". Or, "I feel sad, because I feel alone, hopeless." The lie is "You are alone and hopeless". You don't have to revisit the past to discern the lies you are feeling.

Now, think of a time in which you recently were experiencing a negative emotion or reacting in a way that wasn't filled with the "life and peace" of God. Use the sentences below to help **identify the lies buried in the emotions.**

"I felt _____ **(fill in the blank)**

Why? Because ..._____ (look for the <u>belief</u> in your feelings)

Tips:
*   Don't focus on the circumstances (e.g. I felt sad because she hurt my feelings).
*   Look into the feelings to find what your heart was BELIEVING in those particular circumstances. What was your heart believing at the time? What felt true? (e.g. I felt sad because I felt rejected, unwanted, tossed aside.)

Now, in the space below write in one sentence the LIE that FELT TRUE at that time:

2. **Receive and practice the Truth from Jesus Christ.**
    At this point, it's important to recognize that your feelings and experiences aren't telling you the truth. Jesus is the truth. If you didn't receive it from Jesus, it's not THE TRUTH. What does Jesus say about the lie that has taken authority in your heart? Ask Him. Then listen in

your spirit by faith. Don't merely "figure it out". Turn directly to Jesus Christ who dwells in your spirit. Hold the lie before Him and ask, "Jesus, what do you say about this?" Listen in your heart. Then write down what He brings to mind. Then ask Him again, "What else do you say about this?"

For example, if I wrote, "I am rejected and tossed aside", I would hold this to the Lord, and ask, "What do you say about this Jesus?" and wait for His impression in the Spirit. Immediately I heard, "I am always with you" so I wrote that down. Then I asked again, "What else do you say about this Jesus?" I repeat this process of asking and listening until I get between 5 and 10 really solid words from God about this. I write them all down.

TIPS for RECEIVING TRUTH FROM JESUS:

- When you are receiving the truth from Jesus, don't just think of what you think Jesus would say. Ask Him by faith and look directly to His Spirit within you. Be receptive.
- Sometimes Jesus will give you a "sense" of the truth, a mere impression that you can put into words. Sometimes He will bring words to your mind. Sometimes He may bring a verse or phrase from the Bible to mind. Sometimes He may bring a picture or "mini-movie" to your imagination, etc…
- Initially, don't judge or evaluate what you are receiving, "Is this me or God?" Remember, Jesus lives in you and you CAN hear Him.
- When you are done receiving, then you can evaluate what you received. Jesus doesn't speak English. He speaks TRUTH in LOVE. You can recognize His speaking by the content AND the "tone of voice". Jesus loves you and builds you up. Toss out anything that doesn't align with the truth in Jesus or build you up in love.

IN THE SPACE BELOW-WRITE THE "LIE" YOU IDENTIFIED IN THE PAIN FROM STEP 1:

Now, in the space below, write down what you receive when you ask Jesus directly, "What do you say about this?" Get between 5 to 10 solid words from God about this.

Now what? Use these statements you've received from Jesus to *bring that particular area of your heart* into agreement with God's Spirit. Exercise your FAITH, HOPE, and LOVE as you DECLARE the truth that you just heard from Jesus and contradict the lie.

For example, I may declare "I am not rejected. Jesus, YOU are ALWAYS with Me. You are guarding my future. You have a destiny for me. I have a lot to offer. You've made even my failures and quirks a blessing and a showcase of your glory. Lots of people like me. I am growing stronger every day, etc.."

TIPS FOR RENEWING YOUR MIND:
- Use some of your time alone with God to allow God to point out places your heart that need transformation.
- Use this process for getting free from negative mindsets.
- Once you have a list of 5 to 10 solid impressions from Jesus, use these declarations DAILY for a season as part of your regular time with God to transform that area of your character.
- Don't merely declare God's word with your mind. Exercise your spirit to force your heart to release the troubling lies and embrace the truth.
- Discipline yourself to walk in the truth. Whenever you become aware that you are starting to come under the influence of that same negative lie, simply step back into your spirit and stir up the truths you received from Jesus. In time, you'll be established in the truth and can move on to other areas of transformation.

3. **Forgive others, yourself, and God from the heart.**

Whenever we hold on to an offense, whether from another person, ourselves, or even God, we are giving the power of that offense authority over our lives. Our heart can't embrace God's love while you are holding on to personal offense from the past.

TIPS ON FORGIVENESS:

- Sometimes we need to forgive other people, ourselves, or even God.

- God obviously doesn't do anything wrong. However, many people feel as though God has wronged them, so we must deal with offenses you may hold towards God.

- Forgiveness is NOT saying it wasn't wrong or doesn't matter.

- Forgiveness does NOT depend on the other person. You can forgive someone between yourself and God, even if they aren't sorry or are no longer in contact with you.

- Forgiveness is NOT reconciliation. Forgiveness releases the past offense but it does NOT require a future relationship. That depends on a number of factors, including the character of the other person, your personal safety, etc.

- Forgiveness IS choosing, from the heart, to let the offense go and putting the one who did the wrong into God's hands.

- Unforgiveness only hurts you, not the person with whom you are offended. It gives the wrong they have done continual power over your heart. The only way to break free is to let it go.

- Forgiveness is a deliberate choice from the heart, but it is NOT a feeling. Feelings will follow.

- If you have trouble receiving God's forgiveness for yourself, remember:
    - ✓ holding on to your regret only keeps *you* in bondage to the past
    - ✓ you are giving the past *a continual foothold* in your life.
    - ✓ the *only way to be truly free* is to receive complete forgiveness
    - ✓ punishing yourself *won't change the past* or satisfy God.
    - ✓ Only receiving the gift of forgiveness through Jesus's death satisfies God's requirements for justice and empowers you to become a new person.

With that in mind, ask Jesus, "Who do I need to forgive?" Look to Him directly by faith. Write down the names of the people He shows you.

Now for each person on the list, ask, "What offense do I need to let go?" As the Lord brings things to mind, immediately declare from the heart, "I release them to you. I forgive them. I release this to you Jesus."

Forgiveness FAQ:

1) **What if I forgive, but the event that I have decided to forgive keeps coming back to mind, and sometimes with strong feelings?**

As often as it comes to mind, reaffirm your forgiveness. Sometimes "offense" comes out of our heart all at once. Other times it peels off like an onion.

Also, if you are experiencing strong feelings, you should identify the lie in the pain and receive the truth from Jesus, etc. Sometimes you've let go of the offense, but the painful lie that you received from what happened in the past is still affecting you. For example, if my father hit me with his fist, I can forgive him. But this event may have made me "feel worthless". So even after forgiving him, I may still feel worthless whenever this comes to mind. I need to 1) Identify the Lie in the pain (worthlessness), and 2) Receive the truth from Jesus into my heart. Once you release the lie and receive the truth into your heart in this particular area of your heart, you'll experience freedom.

2) **I suffered more wrongs than I care to remember at the hands of several people. To recall everything they have done is very traumatic and painful. Do I need to revisit the past in order to forgive it?**

No. You need only to forgive from your heart. There is no need to revisit the past. However, if events from the past try to "revisit you" this is the time to deal with them by replacing painful lies with the truth and forgiveness from the heart. There is no need to revisit the past, but there is no reason to carry the painful lies or offenses of the past either.

Through Jesus Christ we can break free from the bondage of the past and walk in newness of life. The practices we've learned in this chapter must be used in combination with other spiritual disciplines that you are learning in this book.

Specifically, it is important to:

1) **Have regular transforming encounters with God. Are you spending time significant time fellowshipping with God enjoying your union with Jesus Christ?** Growing in your experience of the Spirit of God helps believers recognize the difference between old man/carnal mind, and the new man/the mind of the Spirit. The new man in Christ doesn't need inner healing, so as we learn to live in the new man, it often feels like emotional healing.

2) **Govern your own soul and your mouth. Are you rehearsing negativity from the past and imagining the worst for the future, or are you taking every thought and word captive to the truth of God's favor towards you in Christ?** Forget what lies behind and reach forward to what lies ahead, instead of giving your past authority over your life. You set the direction of your life with the words you speak.

ACTIVATION EXERCISES
    1) **Partner Up for ROLE PLAY:**

You have Christian friend over to your house and they share, "I can't stand my roommate. They just bring out the worst in me. I just can't stand being around them. Then I feel bad because I'm the one who ends up acting like jerk. I'm sure they probably hate me too now. I don't know what to do. I can't stand them, and I can't stand myself when I'm around them."

How can you share some of what you've learned in this lesson to help them?

    2) **THIS WEEK, use this process (Identify the Lie in the Pain, Receive the Truth from Jesus and Replace the lies with the Truth, and**

Forgive from the Heart) on yourself with at least one or two more issues.

Describe what happened and your feelings below:

1. **Identify the LIE in the PAIN:**

"I felt <u>(fill in the blank)</u>? _____

Why? (<u>answer)</u>

In the space below write in one sentence the LIE that FELT TRUE at that time:

2. **Receive the truth from Jesus!**
   In the space below, write down what you receive when you ask Jesus directly, "What do you say about this?" Get between 5 to 10 solid impressions you receive from God about this.

Use the truth statements you receive from Jesus for personal declarations of faith on a daily basis until you have become established in truth and freedom.

3. **Forgive others, yourself, and God from the heart.**

   Ask Jesus, "Who do I need to forgive? What offense do I need to let go?"

As the Lord brings things to mind, immediately declare from the heart, "I release them to you. I refuse to hold on to this offense any longer. I release this to you Jesus."

CHAPTER 6
BIOLOGICAL TRANSFORMATION

I.   LOOK BACK-

How have you experienced *God at work in you* as you saturated yourself with the truths that we covered last week in your daily, personal times alone with God?

II.   LESSON

The human race was designed from the beginning as a "two-life-form being". We were created to contain God's Spirit on earth, to "bear the image of God" and "display His likeness", and "exercise dominion over the earth"(Gen. 1:26).

Just like a glove is in the image of a hand so that a hand can be inside of the glove, human beings were designed by God so that He could live inside of us and make His life visible on the earth. We were created with a body to interact with the physical world, a spirit to interface with God, and a soul to allow us to process and respond to what we're experiencing with our spirit and our body. You were specially designed to be God's dwelling place on the earth, the place where He resides and expresses Himself by sharing His life from the inside.

No one is born a Christian. To be a Christian is more than adopting a set of morals and beliefs. The Christian life is fundamentally a matter of biology. If you want to be part of the plant kingdom, you must have plant life. If you want to be part of the monkey kingdom, you must have monkey life. If you want to be part of the lion kingdom, you must have lion life. If you want to be part of the Kingdom of God, you must receive divine life.

In the following Scriptures,

a. UNDERLINE the phrases that indicate that believers in Christ are partaking of **another form of life— God's supernatural life**

b. CIRCLE the phrases that indicate any **abilities or characteristics** of the supernatural life that God gives us.

c. ANSWER any questions based on the verses directly preceding the question.

> *And because you are sons, God has sent the Spirit of his Son into our hearts, crying, "Abba! Father!" (Gal 4:6)*

According to this verse, what is the Spirit of Jesus Christ doing? Where?

The activity of the Spirit of God is like a current in a river, always moving us toward God as a son with trust and love. What does this indicate about *what we can do to* personally cooperate with the life Jesus put inside of us?

> *Jesus answered him, "Truly, truly, I say to you, unless one is born again he cannot see the kingdom of God." Nicodemus said to him, "How can a man be born when he is old? Can he enter a second time into his mother's womb and be born?" Jesus answered, "Truly, truly, I say to you, unless one is born of water and the Spirit, he cannot enter the kingdom of God. That which is born of the flesh is flesh, and that which is born of the Spirit is spirit. Do not marvel that I said to you, 'You must be born again.' (John 3:3-7)*

Select the best answer. According to these verses, when someone is born again of God's Spirit they can
   a) see the Kingdom of God
   b) enter the Kingdom of God
   c) Receive a form of life that didn't come from any human
   d) All of the above

To them God chose to make known how great among the Gentiles are the riches of the glory of this mystery, which is Christ in you, the hope of glory. Him we proclaim, warning everyone and teaching everyone with all wis m, that we may present everyone mature in Christ. For this I toil, struggling with all his energy that he powerfully works within me. (Col 1:27-29)

Based on the verse above, select which ONE of the following is true:

a. Since Christ lives in us, maturity in Christ is easy and automatic.

b. Since Christ lives in us, we can accelerate our growth into maturity in Christ by receiving and living according to the teaching, wisdom, and warnings of the Gospel.

*Examine yourselves, to **see whether you are in the faith**. Test yourselves. Or do you not realize this about yourselves, that **Jesus Christ is in you**?— unless indeed you fail to meet the test!* (2Co 13:5)

Select the best answer. According to this verse, one of the tests that every true Christian must pass is:
   a) **Regular church attendance**
   b) **Daily Bible reading**
   c) **Moral flawlessness**
   d) **That Jesus Christ lives in you**

Select the best answer. This test (whether Jesus Christ is in you) assumes that:
   a) It's impossible for anyone to really know their true spiritual state
   b) It's actually possible for people to experience Jesus Christ Himself living inside of them
   c) Because we can experience Jesus Christ living in us, we can know that our faith is real
   d) B & C

REFLECTION
How have you personally experienced Jesus Christ living inside of you?

SECTION 2- Knowing God by Experiencing His Life

Jesus knew that if He went to the cross, He would be able to give the divine life that He carried inside Himself to all who believe in Him. If He died, anyone in the whole world who wanted to see Him would be able see who He truly was. They would not see Him with their eyes, but because He gives them His own divine life inside of their spirits, they would come to know Jesus *from the inside.*

1) In the following Scriptures,

a. CIRCLE the phrases that indicate that God's **personal indwelling presence gives us ability to truly know Him**

b. ANSWER any questions based on the verses directly preceding the question.

And I (Jesus) will ask the Father, and he will give you another Helper, to be with you forever, even the Spirit of truth, whom the world cannot receive, because it neither sees him nor knows him. You know him, for he dwells with you and will be in you. "I will not leave you as orphans; I will come to you. Yet a little while and the world will see me no more, but you will see me. Because I live, you also will live. In that day you will know that I am in my Father, and you in me, and I in you. Whoever has my commandments and keeps them, he it is who loves me. And he who loves me will be loved by my Father, and I will love him and manifest myself to him." (John 14:16-21)

Select the best answer. According to this verse, through the Holy Spirit, believers can actually experience that:
- a) Jesus Christ is inside of the Father
- b) We are inside of Jesus Christ (who is inside of the Father)
- c) Jesus Christ is inside of us
- d) All of the Above

Jesus said that as we "love Him and keep His commands" we will experience the Father's love and the Son's manifest presence in our life. Why did Jesus believe it was necessary to send the Holy Spirit to make this possible?

By this you know the Spirit of God: every spirit that confesses that Jesus Christ has come in the flesh is from God, and every spirit that does not confess Jesus is not from God. This is the spirit of the antichrist, which you heard was coming and now is in the world already. Little children, you are from God and have overcome them, for he who is in you is greater than he who is in the world. (1Jn 4:2-4)

According to these verses, how does the having the Spirit of God impact what we believe about Jesus Christ?

Will God's Spirit ever contradict God's written Word in the Bible? Why is this important to realize?

Will God's Spirit ever contradict our personal understanding of God's Word? How is that different than actually contradicting the Word of God itself?

And this is eternal life, that they know you the only true God, and Jesus Christ whom you have sent. (John 17:3)

How could you use this verse to help explain the difference between *knowing about God, and actually knowing Him* by participating in His eternal life?

Indeed, I count everything as loss because of the surpassing worth of knowing Christ Jesus my Lord. For his sake I have suffered the loss of all things and count them as rubbish, in order that I may gain Christ and be found in him, not having a righteousness of my own that comes from the law, but that which comes through faith in Christ, the righteousness from God that depends on faith—that I may know him and the power of his resurrection, and may share his sufferings, becoming like him in his death, that by any means possible I may attain the resurrection from the dead... Brothers, I do not consider that I have made it my own. But one thing I do: forgetting what lies behind and straining forward to what lies ahead, I press on toward the goal for the prize of the upward call of God in Christ Jesus. (Php 3:8-14)

According to the previous verses, select whether the statements below are True or False: Knowing Jesus Christ is…

_____ Only possible by forsaking any righteousness of your own and putting your faith completely in Him to be your sole source of righteousness

_____ Achieved through detailed theological study of the original Greek and Hebrew Scriptures

_____ Experienced as we live in the power of His resurrection life and are conformed to His self-sacrificing love

_____ Effortless, easy and automatic for those who believe

_____ Is a lifestyle that requires the wholehearted effort of our entire being in an unrelenting pursuit of personal participation in Christ's presence, power and character

*None of the rulers of this age understood this, for if they had, they would not have crucified the Lord of glory. But, as it is written, "What no eye has seen, nor ear heard, nor the heart of man imagined, what God has prepared for those who love him"—**these things God has revealed to us through the Spirit. For the Spirit searches everything, even the depths of God.** For who knows a person's thoughts except the spirit of that person, which is in him? So also no one comprehends the thoughts of God except the Spirit of God. **Now we have received not the spirit of the world, but the Spirit who is from God, that we might understand the things freely given us by God.** (1Co 2:8-12)*

According to this verse, how does having the Spirit of God in us make it possible for us to understand God?

What insight does this give us about how we can understand God's Word today?

Summary: We must be born again of God's Spirit to know God. Once we receive His Spirit, we can now perceive God's very own perspective, if we just turn to His presence within us by faith. The same Spirit that has given us the Word of God and who lived in Jesus Christ now lives in us.

III. LOOK OUT:

PRACTICE

a. Role Play:

Using some of the truths we covered in today's lesson, practice responding to the following scenarios.

1. Your friend says to you, "I read about the people who thought they were Christians and said, "Lord, Lord" but then Jesus said, "Depart from me" (Mat 7:21), and it really scared me. How can I be sure that this doesn't wind up being me? Is there a way to tell if I'm really in the faith or not?"

2. Your friend says to you, "You seem to really get a lot out of the Bible and church and stuff. It never seems to make sense to me. I don't really connected with all that stuff. What am I missing?"

3. You meet a guy on the beach who boasts about spending a week getting drunk, high, and picking up loose women. You begin to share how Jesus made a huge difference in your life. He responds, "Oh, you don't have to tell me man. I'm with you. I've been a Christian my whole life too." How can you respond by using some of the truths in this lesson?

PLAN

Personal Practice:

Test Yourself- How are you experiencing Jesus Christ in You? This week, as part of your personal times with God, keep a small journal of all the ways that you perceive the presence and activity of Jesus Christ dwelling *inside of you* (**not merely at work in your circumstances**). Be sure to praise and thank Him for His presence in your life.

CHAPTER 7
DOMINION OVER SICKNESS

I. LOOK BACK-
How have you experienced **God at work *in you*** or ***through you*** this past week? Share any highlights, lessons, insights or encouragement, especially from last week's assignment journaling how you experienced "Christ in you".

II. LESSON
In this lesson you will learn how to heal the sick like Jesus Christ.

Some Christians come from backgrounds where they were taught that God no longer intends to work in His miraculous power through believers today, because now we have the Bible. They suppose that miracles were needed only to validate the Bible, and once the Bible's authority is established miracles are no longer needed. Because they hold to this view, anyone who claims that God is working through them to heal the sick is treated with a great deal of suspicion and sometimes outright hostility, since in their view, this would give them authority to speak for God like the original New Testament writers. There's one BIG problem with this though… this view is never taught in the Bible… ***anywhere***! In fact, the Bible specifically teaches otherwise.

SECTION 1- WHO CAN HEAL THE SICK?
1) Read the verses below.
a. UNDERLINE every phrase that indicates WHO God expects to heal the sick or cast out demons
b. CIRCLE any word or phrase that indicates HOW believers minister healing or cast out demons
c. ANSWER the questions following each of the verses below based on the verse immediately above the question.

So Jesus said to them, "Truly, truly, I say to you, the Son can do nothing of his own accord, but only what he sees the Father doing. For whatever the Father does, that the Son does in like manner. John 5:19

Could Jesus do miracles on His own accord?

What did Jesus see the Father doing? Leaving people sick, making people sick, or healing the sick?

A disciple is not above his teacher, but everyone when he is fully trained will be like his teacher. Luke 6:40

What is the end result of being fully trained by Jesus? How does this relate to healing the sick?

Jesus said to him, "...Whoever has seen me has seen the Father. Do you not believe that I am in the Father and the Father is in me?...The Father who dwells in me does his works. Believe me that I am in the Father and the Father is in me, or else believe on account of the works themselves. Truly, truly, I say to you, whoever believes in me will also do the works that I do; and greater works than these will he do, because I am going to the Father." (John 14:9-12)

Since Jesus is our clearest and most complete picture of God, how do we see the Father's response to those who need healing?

Select the best answer. Who does Jesus say will do the same works He did and even greater?
   a) The 12 apostles and first century believers only
   b) Spiritually mature church leaders
   c) Those with a special gift and calling on their lives
   d) Whoever believes in Him

How will someone who truly believes in the same gospel that Jesus taught respond to those who need healing?

Since Jesus said believers will "do the works that I do", which approach should we take towards healing the sick and casting out demons:

a) We should dig around in people's past to find out the spiritual reasons for the condition then take appropriate actions

b) We should ask God to heal them or set them free, then accept whatever results (or lack of results) as the final indication of God's will

c) We should invite them to church and let our pastor handle it

d) We should do what Jesus did- speak and act in compassion and exercise Kingdom authority over the works of darkness to set the captives free

And he said to them, "Go into all the world and proclaim the gospel to the whole creation. Whoever believes and is baptized will be saved… and these signs will accompany those who believe: in my name they will cast out demons; they will speak in new tongues; they will pick up serpents with their hands; and if they drink any deadly poison, it will not hurt them; they will lay their hands on the sick, and they will recover." Mark 16:15-18

Who does Jesus say will have signs following them— apostles, or those who believe what the gospel the apostles preached?

Look over the list of the signs that follow believers. What does this tell us about the content of the apostolic gospel?

According to this Scripture, who must have the faith for healing, the one who is sick or the believer who is laying hands?

Lord, Lord, did we not prophesy in your name, and cast out demons in your name, and do many mighty works in your name?' And Jesus will declare to them, 'I never knew you; depart from me, you workers of lawlessness.' Matt. 7:21-23

What does this teach us about the source of our spiritual identity? Is it miracles through us or Christ in us?

If Jesus doesn't deny that even the unconverted can do miracles in His Name, do you think miracles may also be possible for a true child of God?

But Peter said, "I have no silver and gold, but what I do have I give to you. In the name of Jesus Christ of Nazareth, rise up and walk!" Act 3:6

Did Peter need to ask God to release more power? Or did he believe he had the authority to give to others what God had already given us through Christ?

Was the lame man healed because he had faith or because Peter had faith for his healing?

When Peter saw it he addressed the people: "Men of Israel, why do you wonder at this, or why do you stare at us, as though by our own power or piety we have made him walk? The God of Abraham, the God of Isaac, and the God of Jacob, the God of our fathers, glorified his servant Jesus…And His name--by faith in his name--has made this man strong whom you see and know, and the faith that is through Jesus has given the man this perfect health in the presence of you all. Act 3:11-16

Did Peter attribute his miracles to the fact he was an apostle?

Does he who supplies the Spirit to you and works miracles among you do so by works of the law, or by hearing with faith? Gal 3:5

Did Paul assume that the believers in his churches were experiencing miracles? Why?

How do we experience miracles— by earning them or by exercising faith in Jesus Christ?

And he called the twelve together and gave them power and authority over all demons and to cure diseases, and he sent them out to proclaim the kingdom of God and to heal. (Luke 9:1-2) After this the Lord appointed seventy-two others and sent them on ahead of him, two by two, into every town and place where he himself was about to go. Heal the sick in it and say to them, 'The kingdom of God has come near to you.' (Luke10:1,9)

Did Jesus ever send anyone out to proclaim the gospel with words alone? Why?

When Jesus sent out the 72 after sending out the 12, was He demonstrating that a supernatural life of miracles was exclusive to the 12 apostles or for all His disciples?

And proclaim as you go, saying, 'The kingdom of heaven is at hand.' Heal the sick, raise the dead, cleanse lepers, cast out demons. Mat 10:7-8

Do we need a special leading to obey these things, or can we just act on the authority of the Jesus' commands to His disciples?

Select the best answer. According to this Scripture, the way in which disciples were to heal the sick, raise the dead and cast out demons is:
  a) Very complicated
  b) Very different in approach between healing, deliverance, and dead raising.
  c) Required that you investigate the spiritual background of the person to whom you are ministering in order to discover the spiritual root causes
  d) Simple and basically the same— You exercise the authority and the power of the Kingdom of God to set the captive free

And Jesus came and said to them, "All authority in heaven and on earth has been given to me. Go therefore and make disciples of all nations, baptizing them in the name of the Father and of the Son and of the Holy Spirit, teaching them to observe all that I have commanded you. And behold, I am with you always, to the end of the age." Matt. 28:18-20

Since Jesus command the disciples to heal the sick, cast out demons, and raise the dead, according to Matt. 28:18-20, should disciples be taught to obey these commands today?

If we are obeying the same command, should we do it differently or in the same way?

SECTION 2- Dominion Over Devils
Let's examine the Scriptures regarding believers and the devil.

a. **UNDERLINE** every phrase that indicates the victory and authority believers have over devils
b. **CIRCLE** every phrase that indicates something believers can do to advance the Kingdom of God against devils
c. **ANSWER** the questions following each of the verses below based on the verse immediately above the question.

The seventy-two returned with joy, saying, "Lord, even the demons are subject to us in your name!" And he said to them, "I saw Satan fall like lightning from heaven. Behold, I have given you authority to tread on serpents and scorpions, and over all the power of the enemy, and nothing shall hurt you.
(Luke 10:17-19)
How much authority does God give the devil over believers?

How much authority does God give the believer over devils?

Whoever makes a practice of sinning is of the devil, for the devil has been sinning from the beginning. The reason the Son of God appeared was to destroy the works of the devil. (1Jn 3:8)

What are some of the ways that Jesus destroyed the works of the devil?

Andy Hayner
FullSpeedImpact.com

How can believers destroy works of the devil today?

He disarmed the rulers and authorities and put them to open shame, by triumphing over them in Him (Jesus Christ). (Col 2:15)

Since the devil has been disarmed by Jesus Christ, how should this influence our attitude in spiritual battles?
You prepare a table before me in the presence of my enemies; you anoint my head with oil; my cup overflows. (Psa 23:5)

True or False:

_____ It's always necessary for believers to directly fight the devil.

_____ Even when we are aware that the enemy is present, believers can remain focused on enjoying the finished work of Christ, (feasting at the table God has prepared for us) in the security of God's care.

And these signs will accompany those who believe: in my name they will cast out demons; they will speak in new tongues… (Mark 16:17)

True or False: According to this Scripture…

_____ "Deliverance" is casting out demons by exercising the authority and power we have through our union with Jesus Christ

_____ Casting out demons requires confidence in the fact God has authorized you to speak and act just like Jesus

_____ "Deliverance" is a specialized ministry that requires digging into people's past to discover the spiritual root cause of the demonic oppression. If you don't discover the root cause and deal with that, you won't have the authority to cast the demons out.

_____ We don't need to know how or why the demons came in to be able to get them to go out. They will go out because we have the authority to make them go in Jesus' Name.

_____ We need to know the name of the demon before we can cast it out.

_____ The only name we need to know to cast out a demon is Jesus Christ.

Finally, be strong in the Lord and in the strength of his might. Put on the whole armor of God, that you may be able to stand against the schemes of the devil. For we do not wrestle against flesh and blood, but against the rulers, against the authorities, against the cosmic powers over this present darkness, against the spiritual forces of evil in the heavenly places. Therefore take up the whole armor of God, that you may be able to withstand in the evil day, and having done all, to stand firm…. In all circumstances take up the shield of faith, with which you can extinguish all the flaming darts of the evil one… praying at all times in the Spirit, with all prayer and supplication. To that end keep alert with all perseverance, making supplication for all the saints, (Eph 6:10-18)

For if, because of one man's trespass, death reigned through that one man, much more will those who receive the abundance of grace and the free gift of righteousness **reign in life through the one man Jesus Christ***. (Rom 5:17)*

Summary: Christians walk in union with Jesus Christ. We must renew our minds to adopt His mindset and attitude towards disease and devils. Jesus always treated sickness as a work of the enemy that was subject to Him. In order to minister healing or cast out demons, we speak and act in the authority of Jesus Christ to set the captives free.

III. LOOK OUT
PRACTICE
1. Review the basic outline to healing ministry together. Someone who is experienced should demonstrate each step.

1. Approach
2. Ask
3. Minister
4. Test
5. Rejoice or Repeat
6. Connect and Close

1. **Approach**: Go to people. Build rapport quickly with a pleasant demeanor. Take as much time to building rapport as you feel is appropriate or necessary.

2. **Ask:** Say something like, "I noticed you were walking with a cane and thought, you're too young and good looking to be using a cane. What happened? Do you have pain?" Or, if there is no visible condition like a cane, crutch, or an oxygen tank, you can say, "Do you happen to have anything that causes pain in your body, anything at all? God uses me to set people free from pain and I just felt like I should ask you."

3. **Minister:** Tell them. "I can help you with that. Are you ready for that pain to go?" While holding out your hand like you're asking for money, say "Let me see your hand for a second" They'll put their hand in yours automatically, even if they are wondering what you are about to do. Then grasp their hand firmly (but not hard enough to hurt them), and minister healing, "Father, thank you for all you've done. In Jesus' Name, pain/sickness, Go now. Be healed. I set you free in Jesus' Name"

4. **Test:** Then immediately say, "Now test that out. Move it around and tell me what's changed."

5. **Rejoice or Repeat:** Rejoice in their healing or Repeat the process, by saying, "Sometimes I pray more than once. Let's hit this again quickly." Then take their hands and command healing once more.

6. **Connect and Close:** When it's time to wrap up your spontaneous healing ministry, you will have experienced perceptible change or not. Regardless, maintain your confidence in God and love for people. You may want to offer contact information or additional resources to people who seem open to more.

2. Role Play: Break up in pairs and practice ministering to a stranger with pain. One person should take the role of the infirm person, and the other person takes the role of the minister. Go through this exercise by breaking down the steps and adding one more step each time:

    a. Practice Approach

    b. Approach and Ask

    c. Approach, ask and Minister

    d. Approach, ask, minister, test

    e. Approach, ask, minister, test, rejoice/repeat

    f. Then finally put it all together with a Connect/Close

Each time, you repeat all the previous steps and add one more. This will give you lots of repetition on the early steps, but I've found that the beginning steps are the most important to get comfortable with. The repetition will help you gain confidence and comfort.

Then switch roles and allow your partner to practice going through all the steps.

PLAN

1. Who do you know that has sickness or pain in their body? Make an appointment to go and minister to them.

2. Pick a store and go and minister to as many employees as you can. Approach them and build a little rapport. Then ask them, "You are working hard, and I've found that a lot of people are having to work in spite of how they feel. Do you have anything that gives you pain or trouble at all in your body? Anything at all?" Then take the conversation from there. You can do this with a partner.

Write your plan here:
      Where?
      When?
      With whom?

PRAY

If anyone needs healing or prayer, lay hands and minister to one another.

CHAPTER 8
LIVING IN ETERNITY... NOW
PART 1

I. LOOK BACK-

How have you experienced *God at work in you* and/or *God at work through you to impact people around* you this past week?

II. LESSON

What made Jesus different was that the things that were going on inside of Him did not have its origin in time or space. As His body was in Galilee His inner parts were living *inside of His Father.* Jesus had constant *access realms beyond space and time*, and made them part of His conscious experience on earth through the union of His *human spirit with God.* Although Jesus was designed like us, He had the complete package that included the components that allowed Him to access the Father and display the Father.

What is often less obvious to Christians today is that **this is *the only way* for us to live the Christian life too**— by finding life in unseen realms, outside of space and time *inside of Christ.* Just as Jesus Christ found life by dwelling inside of His Father, we must dwell *inside of Christ.* We must get to know God in heavenly realms. More than this, just as the Man Christ Jesus had to discover His identity through His Father's revelation, we too must discover our true identity in eternity, from our Father, in union with Jesus Christ.

We tend to interpret our experiences based on our five senses. God's eternal perspective is very different than our worldly perspective. This lesson will focus on what God says is true about us because of our union with Jesus Christ.

For ALL of the following Scriptures in this lesson

a) **Underline:** words or phrases that indicate God's eternal perspective
b) **Circle:** any word or phrase that indicates *anything we can do* to experience God's eternal perspective NOW (not every verse has anything to circle)
c) **Answer** any questions.

In God's Eyes

…He chose us in Him before the foundation of the world, that we should be holy and blameless before him. In love he predestined us for adoption as sons through Jesus Christ, according to the purpose of his will, to the praise of his glorious grace, with which he has blessed us in the Beloved. (Eph 1:3-6)

According to this Scripture, which of the following statements may *seem logical*, but is NOT actually what God says in His Word?

a) God chose you to be *like God*- holy and blameless.
b) God chose you to be *with God*- before Him
c) God gave you an amazing destiny- to be adopted as a son to demonstrate the glory of His grace.
d) If we don't make it to heaven, it's God's fault because He must not have chosen us.

True or False?

_____ During his days on the earth, through the Spirit, as a man Jesus Christ discovered and experienced the relationship that His Father had established with Him in eternity.

_____ Before you were ever created, God established a relationship with you in Christ. Through faith in Jesus Christ, we can experience that relationship NOW.

REFLECTION

When Jesus was alive on the earth, how old was He in the Spirit?

Once you receive Jesus Christ and become one Spirit with Him, how old is *the spirit inside of you?*

Think about that as you read...

For those whom he foreknew he also predestined to be conformed to the image of his Son, in order that he might be the firstborn among many brothers. And those whom he predestined he also called, and those whom he called he also justified, and those whom he justified he also glorified. (Rom 8:29-30)

God is beyond the boundaries of time and space in eternal realms. **Based on the verses above, who knew you first, you or God?**

What destiny did God declare for you when He foreknew you?

What is the significance of God saying that you are "glorified"(past tense)?

REFLECTION

Does your view of your destiny match God's view of your destiny?

What mindsets and habits do you need to change in order to start walking in agreement with God's destiny for your life?

*But God, being rich in mercy, because of the great love with which he loved us, even when we were dead in our trespasses, made us alive together with Christ—by grace you have been saved—and **raised us up with him** and **seated us with him in the heavenly places in Christ Jesus**, so that in the coming ages he might show the immeasurable riches of his grace in kindness toward us in Christ Jesus. (Eph. 2:4-7)*

According to the previous Scripture, which of the following statements are NOT what God says in His Word?

a) In God's eyes, you have already been raised from the dead, because you were in Christ when God raised Him up.

b) You are already seated in heaven with Jesus Christ.

c) God's grace and kindness put you in His presence. You are there for God to display His grace!

d) Since God has already seated you in heaven with Christ by grace, it really doesn't matter how you live the remainder of your life on earth.

*So you also must consider yourselves dead to sin and **alive to God in Christ Jesus**... Do not present your members to sin as instruments for unrighteousness, but **present yourselves to God as those who have been brought from death to life**, and your members to God as instruments for righteousness. (Rom 6:13)*

What does it mean to consider yourself "alive to God in Christ Jesus" and to "present yourself to God as those who have been brought from death to life"?

What are some of the challenges you have had to overcome to make it your lifestyle to relate to God *exclusively* on the basis of how He sees us in Christ?

*And because **you are sons**, God has sent the Spirit of his Son into our hearts, crying, "Abba! Father!" So **you are no longer a slave, but a son, and if a son**, then an heir through God. (Gal 4:6-7)*

*Therefore be imitators of God, as **beloved children**. (Eph. 5:1)*

*God is faithful, by whom **you were called into the fellowship of his Son**, Jesus Christ our Lord. (1Co 1:9)*

What do the Scriptures in this section indicate about how God feels about you?

Have you truly taken this to heart in the way you relate to God?

True or False?

_____ God's grace doesn't really empower you to be like Him. He just tells us these things so that we will feel emotionally secure even though we continually fall into sin.

_____ God has called you to enjoy the same relationship His Son has with Him by direct spiritual participation in the Son's Spirit... now and forever.

_____ It's irreverent and prideful to believe that God would give us the same relationship with Him that Jesus Christ enjoys.

*Therefore, since **we have been justified by faith**, we have peace with God through our Lord Jesus Christ. Through him we have also obtained access by faith into this grace in which we stand, and we rejoice in hope of the glory of God. (Rom 5:1-2)*

Note: "Justified" = declared completely righteous, just as if you've always done everything that has ever been required

Read the verse above by replacing the word "justified" with its definition.

*He has **now** reconciled in his body of flesh by his death, in order to present you **holy and blameless and above reproach before him**, (Col 1:22)*

*For our sake he made him to be sin who knew no sin, so that **in him we might be made the righteousness of God**. (2Co 5:17-21)*

*For by a single offering **he has perfected for all time** those who are being sanctified. (Heb. 10:14)*

True or False?

_____ Jesus Christ has made you blameless and above reproach in the sight of God.

_____ Nobody is perfect, because everyone makes mistakes.

_____ Even while we grow to become more sanctified, God has already perfected us eternally because of the death of Christ for us.

_____ You are still just a sinner saved by grace.

_____ You aren't just forgiven. God makes you as righteous as Jesus Christ.

Let's declare these truths together: "Because of my union with Jesus Christ, I am holy. I am blameless. I am above reproach. I have been made the righteousness of God. I am perfected for all time. I am being sanctified, set apart to walk in all Christ's perfections."

*When **Christ who is your life** appears, then **you also will appear with him in glory**. (Col 3:4)*

True or False?

_____ God says that Christ is your life.

_____ God is right about Christ being your life, no matter how you feel.

REFLECTION

What do people typically base their perceptions of themselves upon?

What are some of the things that you do that help you to come into agreement with God and recognize that Christ, who lives inside you, is your life?

Believers and Blessings

*Blessed be the God and Father of our Lord Jesus Christ, who hath **blessed us with all spiritual blessings** in heavenly places in Christ: (Eph. 1:3)*

True or False?

_____ God is going to bless you once you get your breakthrough.

_____ God has already blessed you because Christ has gotten your breakthrough.

_____ You still need to pay preachers money to be blessed.

_____ We don't give money to get blessings. We give because we are already blessed and we want to spread our blessings, exercise our faith in God, and show God's love to people.

_____ Even though you are a born again believer, you might be cursed.

_____ If you are a born again believer, you are blessed. You can't be cursed. Christ became a curse for you (Gal. 3:13), and no one can curse whom God has blessed (Num. 23:8).

Believers and The Devil

> *Behold, **I give unto you authority to tread on serpents and scorpions, and over __all__ the power of the enemy**: and **nothing** shall by any means hurt you. (Luke 10:19)*

> *…God raised him (Jesus Christ) from the dead and seated him at his right hand in the heavenly places, **far above all rule and authority and power and dominion, and above every name that is named**, not only in this age but also in the one to come. And **he put all things under his feet and gave him as head over all things to the church, which is his body, the fullness of him who fills all in all**. (Eph. 1:19-23)*

True or False?

_____ Jesus gives each of His disciples authority over all the devil's power.

_____ Because of union with Jesus Christ, wherever a believer goes, they outrank every demon they may meet.

_____ The devil only has power but has no legitimate authority to harm a believer.

_____ Every devil you meet is already defeated by Jesus Christ.

III. LOOK OUT

PRACTICE

A. Partner up for Role Play. Practice responding to the following scenarios:

1. You are invited out to dinner after church. The main point of the pastor's sermon was, "We are all just sinners, saved by grace." Your friend asked what you thought of the sermon. You say, "Well, I don't really agree with the main point." They say, "Really? Why?"

   Respond by using some of the truths you've learned in this lesson.

2. You have a Christian friend who comes over to your house fresh from a spiritual warfare and deliverance conference. She proceeds to tell you that she's honestly quite worried that she's under a "generational curse" because her grandfather was a Hindu. She's not sure how this is impacting her, but you can tell she's quite unsettled.

   Respond by using some of the truths you've learned in this lesson.

PLAN

Assignment

Using the Scriptures in this lesson, write out ALL the things that God says are true about you in Jesus Christ. Use a dictionary to look up any words that you'd like more insight about. Make these statements your DAILY declaration, with thanks and praise to God.

Because Christ lives in me, and He is my life, I am...

CHAPTER 9
CULTIVATING A LIFESTYLE
OF FELLOWSHIP WITH GOD

I. LOOK BACK

How have you experienced *God at work in you* and/or *God at work through you to impact people around* you this past week?

II. LESSON

HABITS TO CULTIVATE A LIFESTYLE OF FELLOWSHIP WITH GOD

While it is crucial to have regular times alone with God, we don't want to compartmentalize God to our prayer times. God has removed the separation between "secular" and "spiritual." Our entire lives, "whether we eat or drink, or whatever we do" is now part of our relationship with God. It's all included into our fellowship with God. God is always with us so we can now walk with God. Our lives are immersed in God. When we work, "we work as unto the Lord." Every relationship, whether within our family, or friends, neighbors or even persecutors, has now become an opportunity to live in fellowship with God.

In this lesson we will introduce spiritual habits that we can nurture to cultivate lifestyle of fellowship with God.

1) Have times devoted to personal communion with God every day.
2) Make each day a running conversation with God.
3) Call on the Name of the Lord, Rejoice and give thanks to God continually.
4) Pray in tongues.
5) Offer your activities to God as worship by faith.

In the Scriptures below:
a. UNDERLINE instructions about HOW, WHEN, or WHERE we can pray.
b. CIRCLE the benefits and results of cultivating a lifestyle of fellowship with God.

But when you pray, go into your room and shut the door and pray to your Father who is in secret. And your Father who sees in secret will reward you. "And when you pray, do not heap up empty phrases as the Gentiles do, for they think that they will be heard for their many words. Do not be like them, for your Father knows what you need before you ask him. (Mat 6:6-8)

Lead me in your truth and teach me, for you are the God of my salvation; for you I wait all the day long. Psalm 25:5

Pray without ceasing. 1 Thes. 5:17

praying at all times in the Spirit, with all prayer and supplication. To that end keep alert with all perseverance, making supplication for all the saints, Eph 6:18

But stay awake at all times, praying that you may have strength to escape all these things that are going to take place, and to stand before the Son of Man." Luke 21:36

Because you are sons, God has sent the Spirit of his Son into our hearts, crying, "Abba! Father!"
Gal. 4:5-6

Does the Spirit of Jesus Christ ever stop fellowshipping with the Father inside of you?

How does this make continual fellowship with God a practical experience that empowers us rather than a frustrating impossibility?

How can that help us understand true prayer? Is it something we do, or something we become aware of and participate in?

SECTION 2- Calling, Rejoice, and Giving Thanks.

In the Scriptures below:
   a. **UNDERLINE** any instructions about HOW, WHEN, or WHERE we can call on the Name of the Lord, Rejoice, and/or Give Thanks
   b. **CIRCLE** any benefits and results of cultivating a lifestyle of fellowship with God.

To the church of God that is in Corinth, to those sanctified in Christ Jesus, called to be saints together with all those who in every place call upon the name of our Lord Jesus Christ, both their Lord and ours. (1 Cor. 1:2)

So flee youthful passions and pursue righteousness, faith, love, and peace, along with those who call on the Lord from a pure heart. (2 Tim.2:22)

… For the same Lord is Lord of all, bestowing his riches on all who call on him. (Rom 10:12)

For you, O Lord, are good and forgiving, abounding in steadfast love to all who call upon you… In the day of my trouble I call upon you, for you answer me.. (Psalm 86:5,7)

…No one can say "Jesus is Lord" (authentically) *except in the Holy Spirit.* (1Co 12:3) Note: In the context, the apostle Paul is pointing out an alternative to speaking in tongues for the church to stir up the operation of the Holy Spirit when they meet corporately.

What did you learn about the benefits of a calling upon the Name of the Lord from the verses above?

What is the difference between "calling on the Lord" as a "spiritual orphan" vs. the way in which we call on the Lord as His own children?

Rejoice in the Lord always; again I will say, rejoice. (Php 4:4)

Rejoice always, pray without ceasing, give thanks in all circumstances; for this is the will of God in Christ Jesus for you. (1Th 5:16-18)

Do not be slothful in zeal, be fervent in spirit, serve the Lord. Rejoice in hope, be patient in tribulation, be constant in prayer. (Rom 12:11-12)

Through him we have also obtained access by faith into this grace in which we stand, and we rejoice in hope of the glory of God. Not only that, but we rejoice in our sufferings, knowing that suffering produces endurance…character,… and hope, and hope does not put us to shame, because God's love has been poured into our hearts through the Holy Spirit who has been given to us. (Rom 5:2-5)

And whatever you do, in word or deed, do everything in the name of the Lord Jesus, giving thanks to God the Father through him. (Col 3:17)

Therefore, as you received Christ Jesus the Lord, so walk in him, rooted and built up in him and established in the faith, just as you were taught, overflowing with gratitude. (Col 2:6-7)

Based on the Scriptures above, what is the relationship between rejoicing, thanksgiving, our circumstances, and our relationship with God?

SECTION 3- Tongues
In the Scriptures below:
   a. **UNDERLINE** any instructions about WHO God wants to speak in tongues
   b. **CIRCLE** any benefit or result of speaking in tongues

And these signs will accompany those who believe: in my name they will cast out demons; they will speak in new tongues; (Mar 16:17)

According to Jesus, who can experience the operation of tongues in their lives? Those with a special gift? Or those who believe the message He entrusted to the apostles?

For one who speaks in a tongue speaks not to men but to God; for no one understands him, but he utters mysteries in the Spirit...The one who speaks in a tongue builds up himself...Now I want you all to speak in tongues... I thank God that I speak in tongues more than all of you. (1Co 14:2-5,18)

What are some of the reasons that praying in tongues should be a powerful part of our Christian life?

REFLECTION

For a variety of reasons, many believers have concluded "tongues is NOT for me". Does your attitude towards speaking in tongues align with God's Word, that says, "I *want* you ALL to speak in tongues" and with Jesus who said that "speaking in new tongues" is a sign that "*will* accompany *those who believe*"?

SECTION 4- Presenting Your Activities as Worship

In the Scriptures below:

    a. **CIRCLE** any activities that can be offered as Worship to God

Bondservants, obey in everything those who are your earthly masters, not by way of eye-service, as people-pleasers, but with sincerity of heart, fearing the Lord. Whatever you do, work heartily, as for the Lord and not for men, knowing that from the Lord you will receive the inheritance as your reward. You are serving the Lord Christ. (Col 3:22-24)

"Whoever receives one such child in my name receives me, and whoever receives me, receives not me but him who sent me." (Mar 9:37)

"I appeal to you therefore, brothers, by the mercies of God, to present your bodies as a living sacrifice, holy and acceptable to God, which is your spiritual worship." (Rom 12:1)

But on some points I have written to you very boldly by way of reminder, because of the grace given me by God to be a minister of Christ Jesus to the Gentiles in the priestly service of the gospel of God, so that the offering of the Gentiles may be acceptable, sanctified by the Holy Spirit. (Rom 15:15-16)

For I was hungry and you gave me food, I was thirsty and you gave me drink, I was a stranger and you welcomed me, I was naked and you clothed me, I was sick and you visited me, I was in prison and you came to me.' Then the righteous will answer him, saying, 'Lord, when did we see you hungry and feed you, or thirsty and give you drink? And when did we see you a stranger and welcome you, or naked and clothe you? And when did we see you sick or in prison and visit you?' And the King will answer them, 'Truly, I say to you, as you did it to one of the least of these my brothers, you did it to me.' (Mat 25:35-40)

REFLECTION
How would offering specific activities that you are doing as worship to God impact your outlook and attitude?

III. LOOK OUT
PLAN
1. This week you will begin to cultivate a lifestyle of fellowship with God by developing the habits we discussed in this lesson. Read the "Tips" below.

Tips for Cultivating a Lifestyle of Fellowship with God:
- Manage your wake and bed times. Reduce your "media time".
- Make your "drive time" worship and prayer time.
- Make the most of mundane tasks by stirring up your spirit with God.
- As you walk from one place to another, walk with God.
- As you "think" about people or situations, instead of "talking to yourself" talk it over with God.

- Don't put pressure on yourself. God is not an "insecure boyfriend". who needs your constant attention. Turning our hearts. towards God gives Him great pleasure and strengthens our souls.

a. **Discussion: What stands out to you from this lesson as an opportunity to strengthen your fellowship with God as a lifestyle?**

b. If you haven't already, make a plan for DAILY private times alone in communion with God. For many, the starting and/or ending every day with God works best. Make "appointments with God" and keep them. God will be there. Will you?

Write the details about your appointment for time alone with God below:

When?
Where?
How Long?

c. Make each day a running conversation with the Lord. Purpose to cultivate a lifestyle of communion with God by cultivating a different aspect of your fellowship with God each day for the next week:

Day 1- Call on the Name of the Lord
Day 2- Rejoice in the Lord
Day 3- Give thanks
Day 4- Speak in tongues.
Day 5- Offer your Actions as Worship
Day 6- Put them all together.

d. Be prepared to share highlights next week.

PRAY

a. Pray for one another. Ask God to make you a people of continual fellowship with Him and awareness of His presence.

b. If anyone needs healing or prayer, lay hands and minister to one another.

CHAPTER 10
LIVING IN ETERNITY... NOW
PART 2

I. LOOK BACK

How have you experienced *God at work in you* and/or *God at work through you to impact people around* you this past week?

II. LESSON

A child of God hears and obeys His commands in the power of the Holy Spirit. It's our nature. If we fail to obey, it's because we are violating our new nature and failing to use the grace, power, and freedom that God has given us in Christ. God's commands are good— to love God and our neighbors, to set the captives free, to live with integrity and generosity.

However, Jesus Christ accomplished a major step forward in God's plan. He bypassed everything in the entire Old Covenant system to bring us directly into spiritual union with God. Our relationship with God is no longer based on our own "legal record" but upon our spiritual union with Jesus Christ through faith. In Christ, believers are free from any obligation to the Old Covenant Law. Yet, we are not lawless. When faith in Jesus Christ rules in us, so does His Spirit, which unleashes the power of God to operate within us. This empowers us to obey the commands of Jesus Christ by nature in a lifestyle of love and faith that impacts the world.

SECTION 1- Believers and the Old Covenant Law

For ALL of the following Scriptures:

  a) **Underline:** words or phrases that indicate the *believers relationship with the Old Covenant Law*
  b) **Circle:** any word or phrase that indicates *the things that should govern and direct the conduct of the believer's daily life.*
  c) **Answer** any questions.

*For **through the law I died to the law, so that I might live to God**. I have been crucified with Christ. It is no longer I who live, but Christ who lives in me. And the life I now live in the flesh **I live by faith in the Son of God**, who loved me and gave himself for me. (Gal 2:19-20)*

*Now we know that the law is good, if one uses it lawfully, understanding this, that **the law is not laid down for the just** but for the lawless and disobedient, for the ungodly and sinners, for the unholy and profane, for those who strike their fathers and mothers, for murderers, the sexually immoral, men who practice homosexuality, enslavers, liars, perjurers, and whatever else is contrary to sound doctrine, in accordance with the gospel of the glory of the blessed God with which I have been entrusted. (1Ti 1:5-11)*

*__**Y**ou also have died to the law__ through the body of Christ, **so that you may belong to another, to him who has been raised from the dead, in order that we may bear fruit for God**... But **now we are released from the law**, having died to that which held us captive, **so that we serve in the new way of the Spirit** and not in the old way of the written code. (Rom 7:4,6)*

Let me ask you only this: Did you receive the Spirit by works of the law or by hearing with faith? Are you so foolish? Having begun by the Spirit, are you now being perfected by the flesh? Did you suffer so many things in vain—if indeed it was in vain? Does he who supplies the Spirit to you and works miracles among you do so by works of the law, or by hearing with faith—just as Abraham "believed God, and it was counted to him as righteousness"? (Gal 3:2-6)

For his sake I have suffered the loss of all things (specifically Paul's religious accomplishments apart from Christ— see the context) *and count them as rubbish, in order that I may gain Christ and be found in him, not having a righteousness of my own that comes from the law, but that which comes through faith in Christ, the righteousness from God that depends on faith— that I may know him and the power of his resurrection, and may share his sufferings, becoming like him in his death, that by any means possible I may attain the resurrection from the dead. (Php 3:8-11)*

Jesus said, "Whoever has my commandments and keeps them, he it is who loves me. And he who loves me will be loved by my Father, and I will love him and manifest myself to him." (John 14:21)

According to the previous passages above, which of the following statements are NOT true?

a) Christians have the same relationship with the Old Testament Law as a dead man. You have died to the Law. It has no jurisdiction over you.

b) Christians have the same relationship with the Law as the resurrected Jesus Christ. In Him, we are free from the Law, but not lawless because we are governed by the indwelling Spirit of God.

c) The Law of God remains in force for the unjust and sinner. However, it was not given as rules to the new creation. The new creation is ruled directly by the person of the Holy Spirit living within us.

d) Christians can live unto God standing in the righteousness of Christ by faith, and at the same time live unto the Law seeking to establish their own righteousness.

According to these Scriptures, what should govern the behavior of a believer? Place an X in the blank(s) below next to the things that are correct.

_____ the Old Covenant Law	_____ the commandments of Jesus
_____ our faith in Jesus Christ	_____ the Spirit of God within us
_____ our love for Jesus Christ	_____ traditions and professional clergy
_____ our personal views	_____ cultural expectations

Summary: Not only do we start with faith in Jesus Christ. *We walk* by faith in Him. He has fulfilled the requirements of the Old Covenant Law on our behalf. We are no longer on probation. Through Him, we have been brought into living union with God. We must give up a "law based mindset". Believers do God's will, not to earn a relationship or establish right standing with God, but *because we are already His children brought into right standing through Christ by grace.* God has given us a right heart, filled with His Spirit. Because of this, to love God and do His will comes natural to our new nature!

SECTION 2- Your Window to See Eternal Realms

We don't throw out the Old Testament. No! The entire Bible is God's Word and relevant to our lives today. Not because we are part of the Old Covenant bound to the Laws of Moses, but because it is a revelation of the all the fullness of God in Christ Jesus... which is also now inside of us. Instead of merely reading the Bible for personal advice or better theology, we should use the Scriptures from the as a sure revelation to see and explore eternal realities.

Read the following together.

*Jesus said, "You **search the Scriptures** because you think that in them you have eternal life; and it is they that **bear witness about me**, yet you refuse to **come to me** that **you may have life**."* John 5:39-40

According to Jesus, the purpose of the Scriptures is to:
1. Show us Jesus Christ- (all the fullness of God that is in Him, His character, what He has done, etc.)

2. So that we can come to Him and Encounter Him personally, and

3. Receive the Life that is in Him as our Life. We literally can soak the life that is in Him into our souls by faith through His Spirit.

This gives us a basic model of how God wants us to use the Bible to nurture and guide our experience of eternal reality. In every Scripture, we should use the Scriptures to SEE who God is, to SAVOR fellowship with God and to SOAK up His Spirit so we live in His power and love and SPEAK what God says.

1. *SEE- And we all, with unveiled face, beholding the glory of the Lord as in a mirror, are being transformed into the same image from one degree of glory to another. For this comes from the Lord who is the Spirit. (2Co 3:18)*

2. *& 3. SAVOR & SOAK "Because you are sons, God has sent the Spirit of his Son into our hearts, crying, "Abba! Father!""*

4. *SPEAK- Since we have the same spirit of faith according to what has been written, "I believed, and so I spoke," we also believe, and so we also speak, (2Co 4:13)*

Read the following Principles of Christ-centered Revelation. Then read the Scriptures that follow and match the number for each principle with the verse Scripture that supports that principle.

Principles of Christ-centered Revelation
(Match Each one with the correct Scripture that Follow)

1. Jesus Christ is true spiritual reality of every good thing, including food, drink, festivals, Sabbaths, and new moons.

2. Wherever you see any righteousness, sanctification, wisdom, power, or redemption, you are seeing an aspect of what is fully realized in Jesus Christ.

3. The ultimate fulfillment of the priestly ministry, sacrificial offerings, and the true temple is Jesus Christ.

4. Wherever you see God's grace, God's truth, or any aspect of His glory, you are seeing the fullness that is in Jesus Christ.

5. All of the requirements of the Law of Moses are a picture of the life and work that is fully realized in Jesus Christ.

6. Whenever you see genuine Christian living, you are seeing Jesus Christ express Himself by living through His people.

FILL IN THE PROPER NUMBER FROM THE PRECEEDING LIST

_____ *I have been crucified with Christ. It is no longer I who live, but Christ who lives in me. And the life I now live in the flesh I live by faith in the Son of God, who loved me and gave himself for me. (Gal 2:20)*

_____ *but to those who are called, both Jews and Greeks, Christ is the power of God and the wisdom of God… And because of him you are in Christ Jesus, who became to us wisdom from God, righteousness and sanctification and redemption, (1Co 1:24,30)*

_____ *Therefore let no one pass judgment on you in questions of food and drink, or with regard to a festival or a new moon or a Sabbath. These are a shadow of the things to come, but the substance is of Christ. (Col 2:16-17)*

_____ *"Do not think that I have come to abolish the Law or the Prophets; I have not come to abolish them but to fulfill them. (Mat 5:17)*

_____ *For since the law has but a shadow of the good things to come instead of the true form of these realities, it can never, by the same sacrifices that are continually offered every year, make perfect those who draw near… And every priest stands daily at his service, offering repeatedly the same sacrifices, which can never take away sins. But when Christ had offered for all time a single sacrifice for sins, he sat down at the right hand of God, (Heb 10:1,11-12)*

_____ *For the law was given through Moses; grace and truth came through Jesus Christ. No one has ever seen God; the only God, who is at the Father's side, he has made him known. (Joh 1:17-18)[4]*

Summary: The Law puts people on probation until demands are fulfilled. Christ fulfilled the Law on our behalf! The gospel puts you in Christ and Christ in you to empower you to live in God's fullness. Through union with Jesus Christ, you have a new nature that loves God. You are dead to the Law and alive to God to live in His presence and power. You are no longer on probation. God sees you from the vantage point of eternity according to your

---

[4] 6= Gal 2:20, 2= 1 Cor. 1:24,30, 1=Col. 2:16-17, 5=Mt. 5:17, 3= Heb. 10:1,11-12, 4=Jn.1:17-18

spirit which is in union with Jesus Christ.

God wants us to use the Scriptures primarily for personal fellowship, not merely getting personal advice or theological information. In the Scriptures, we have a clear revelation of Jesus Christ and all the fullness of God in Him… which is now inside of us. By God's Word, we can clearly see eternal realities.

III. LOOK OUT

PRACTICE

A. Partner up for Role Play. Practice responding to the following scenarios:

1. You and your Christian friend are hanging out and decide to go grab a bite to eat. Over lunch, your friend says, "I really need to talk with you. If you claim to follow God, you need to stop eating pork because God forbids it."

   How can you use some of the truths in this lesson to help respond to your friend to explain why you are free to eat your bacon double cheese burger for lunch without making God mad at you?

B. GROUP EXERCISE:

As a group, use the Principles of Christ-Centered Revelation to practice
1. SEEING Jesus Christ in the following Scriptures, and
2. SEEING Jesus Christ as YOUR INDWELLING LIFE.

In other words, for each of the following Scriptures, ask, "How does this show me something of the fullness of God that is in Jesus Christ?" and then, "Since Christ is my life, what does this say about who I am in Christ?"

For example:
Love is patient and kind; love does not envy or boast; it is not arrogant (1Co 13:4)

1. Jesus, you are perfect love. You are patient. You are kind. You are not envious or boastful. You are generous and self-less. You do all things

for the glory of Your Father.

Jesus, you dwell inside of me. We are one spirit. You are my perfect love. In You, I am patient. I am Kind. I am not envious or boastful. I am not arrogant. I am a blessing, overflowing with your Spirit.

Love does not rejoice at wrongdoing, but rejoices with the truth. Love bears all things, believes all things, hopes all things, endures all things. (1Co 13:6-7)

1. Jesus, you...

2. Because I am one Spirit with Jesus, I...

O LORD, who shall dwell in your tent? Who shall dwell on your holy hill? He who walks blamelessly and does what is right and speaks truth in his heart; who does not slander with his tongue and does no evil to his neighbor, nor takes up a reproach against his friend; (Psa. 15:1-3)

1. Jesus, you...

2. Because I am one Spirit with Jesus, I...

Trust in the LORD with all your heart, and do not lean on your own understanding. In all your ways acknowledge him, and he will make straight your paths. Be not wise in your own eyes; fear the LORD, and turn away from evil. It will be healing to your flesh and refreshment to your bones. (Prov. 3:5-8)

1. Jesus, you... (Hint: Does Jesus trust His Father?)

2. Because I am one Spirit with Jesus, I...

Know this, my beloved brothers: let every person be quick to hear, slow to speak, slow to anger; for the anger of man does not produce the righteousness of God. (Jas 1:19-20)

1. Jesus, you… (Hint: Is Jesus Christ a good listener?)

2. Because I am one Spirit with Jesus, I…

For some, this exercise can seem a little "cerebral". However, once you develop the ability to see Jesus Christ and to see your life in Him in the Scriptures, then the entire Bible becomes an amazing menu to "taste and see that the Lord is good." The power of this approach is not merely in the SEEING. It's in the tasting! The Bible becomes a launching pad into spiritual encounters with God that will transform your life as you learn to take the things you see and turn your heart to the Lord in praise, love, and thanksgiving.

Make this your lifelong practice!

PLAN

This week, incorporate this approach to using the Scriptures as a revelation of Jesus Christ and our life in Him in your personal fellowship with God.

Begin to use the Bible to fellowship with God, to nurture and guide your experience of eternal reality. In every Scripture, we should use the Scriptures:
1) to SEE who God is
2) to SAVOR fellowship with God- Praise, thank, and love God!
3) to SOAK up His Spirit into our souls to be our life- believe, receive, and surrender.
4) to SPEAK what God says- Make declarations of faith based on the Word of God!

Be prepared to share a highlight or two next week.

CHAPTER 11
EMBODYING THE LOVE OF GOD

I. LOOK BACK-
How have you experienced **God at work** *in you* or *through you* this past week? Each one should share at least one highlight from last week's assignment. How did you experience God SEEING, SAVORING, SOAKING, and SPEAKING from the word?

II. LESSON
You are God's image bearer, created to exercise spiritual dominion on earth and to demonstrate His likeness by living in spiritual union with Him. God doesn't take over and make you His automaton. **He works** *within you* **so that** *you* **can walk this out**. God's plan to demonstrate His character and Kingdom on earth is you, the born again believer.

In this lesson, we will examine ways that we can manifest the image of God and advance the Kingdom.

SECTION 1- Bearing God's Image of Perfect Love

Let's examine the Scriptures.
a. UNDERLINE every phrase that indicates any way in which we can manifest the image of God's perfect love
b. CIRCLE every phrase that indicates the spiritual impact of manifesting His image
c. ANSWER the questions following each of the verses below based on the verse immediately above the question.

A new commandment I give to you, that you love one another: just as I have loved you, you also are to love one another. By this all people will know that you are my disciples, if you have love for one another." (John 13:34-35)

Based on this verse, when people don't treat us right, what reasons do we have to walk in God's love?

Beloved, let us love one another, for love is from God, and whoever loves has been born of God and knows God. Anyone who does not love does not know God, because God is love. (1Jn 4:7-8)

Based on this verse, when people don't treat us right, how is it possible to continue to walk in God's love?

Whoever confesses that Jesus is the Son of God, God abides in him, and he in God. So we have come to know and to believe the love that God has for us. God is love, and whoever abides in love abides in God, and God abides in him. By this is love perfected with us, so that we may have confidence for the day of judgment, because as he is so also are we in this world. There is no fear in love, but perfect love casts out fear. For fear has to do with punishment, and whoever fears has not been perfected in love. We love because he first loved us. If anyone says, "I love God," and hates his brother, he is a liar; for he who does not love his brother whom he has seen cannot love God whom he has not seen. And this commandment we have from him: whoever loves God must also love his brother. (1Jn 4:15-21)

Based on these verses, when people don't treat us right, what reasons do we have to walk in God's love?

REFLECTION

Does any situation have the ability keep you from living in the love of God if you will persevere in faith?

Complete this sentence. Genuine love looks like...

Three times in this section we've given reasons to walk in love even when people don't treat us right. What can we do to live by the wisdom of the gospel instead of allowing darkness in others to become darkness in us?

SECTION 2- Ambassadors of Jesus Christ

Read the Scriptures below.

a. **UNDERLINE** every phrase that refers to the LOVE OF GOD

b. **CIRCLE** every phrase that indicates the MINDSETS and MINISTRY that corresponds to living in the love of God

c. **ANSWER** the questions following each of the verses below based on the verse immediately above the question.

For the love of Christ controls us, because we have concluded this: that one has died for all, therefore all have died; and he died for all, that those who live might no longer live for themselves but for him who for their sake died and was raised. From now on, therefore, we regard no one according to the flesh. Even though we once regarded Christ according to the flesh, we regard him thus no longer... All this is from God, who through Christ reconciled us to himself and gave us the ministry of reconciliation; that is, in Christ God was reconciling the world to himself, not counting their trespasses against them, and entrusting to us the message of reconciliation. Therefore, we are ambassadors for Christ, God making his appeal through us. We implore you on behalf of Christ, be reconciled to God. (2Co 5:14-20)

Select the best answer. Based on the Scripture above, what determines our outlook towards other people?

    a) How they treat us

    b) What they can do for us

    c) What other people might think about us if we step out of cultural expectations

    d) The love of Christ and His finished work on behalf of the world

    e) The responsibility and authority Jesus Christ has entrusted to us

    f) D & E

Select the best answer. When the Love of God controls us...

    a) We won't do anything that could possibly offend someone else

    b) We are no longer controlled by the opinions and fear of man

    c) We reconcile people to God as ambassadors of Jesus Christ

    d) B & C

Andy Hayner
FullSpeedImpact.com

REFLECT

An ambassador acts and speaks on behalf of the one whom they represent.
What steps can you take to become a more effective ambassador?

Walk in wisdom toward outsiders (people who aren't in the Kingdom), *making the most of every opportunity. Let your speech always be gracious, seasoned with salt, so that you may know how you ought to respond to each person. (Col 4:3-6)*
What kind of lifestyle does God say is a walk of "wisdom toward outsiders"?

REFLECT

On a practical level, what does mean to you to have speech *always* seasoned with grace towards people outside the Kingdom?

What are some things you can do to add more "grace seasoning" to your speech?

The goal of our instruction is love that issues from a pure heart and a good conscience and a sincere faith. (1Ti 1:5)

Select the best answer. Based on this verse, the goal of our lives and every moment of our lives is:
    a) To get God's blessings
    b) To have an enjoyable life
    c) To have a powerful ministry
    d) To become the living expression of God's love on earth

If we recognize we need to grow in love, how does this verse help us identify some underlying areas we should address with the gospel in our lives?

REFLECTION

Why does being self-conscience hinder Christ-like love?

How does faith in Christ set us free from self-consciousness and empower us to show Christ's love?

Why is showing Christ's love the inevitable overflow of true faith in Christ?

III. LOOK OUT
PRACTICE
A. Discuss ways that make the most of every opportunity by filling your speech with God's grace in these common, everyday scenarios:

1. Going through the checkout line, speaking to the cashier.

2. Meeting a stranger in a store.

3. Finishing up a meal with a waiter/waitress.

4. Someone you know greets you and asks, "How are you today?"

B. Partner up for role play.

Practice encountering people with grace in each of the scenarios above. Respond to them appropriately to make the most of every opportunity.

PLAN
1. Purpose to unleash the Kingdom of God as part of your everyday lifestyle by speaking to people with grace, encouragement, and God's love.

a. Make it a point to advance the Kingdom each day every time you go out from your own house. Purpose to start conversations. Offer to pray for people. Speak spontaneous words of encouragement to them, etc. Engage the people around you with God's grace.

b. Be prepared to share a few highlights from your experience next week

CHAPTER 12
LOOK WHO'S TALKING

I. LOOK BACK-
How have you experienced **God at work** *in you* or ***through you*** this past week? Share any highlights, lessons, insights or encouragement.

II. LESSON
One of the most powerful elements of Jesus' life and ministry was the confidence He had which came from hearing His Father clearly. Good news! If you are born again, you too can hear God's voice, guaranteed. Christ who now dwells in your spirit gives you a naturally supernatural ability to hear God. In this lesson we will learn more about hearing God.

SECTION 1- HEARING GOD
Read the Scriptures below.

a. UNDERLINE every phrase that indicates WHO can hear God

b. ANSWER the questions following each of the verses below based on the verse immediately above the question.

My sheep hear my voice, and I know them, and they follow me. (Joh 10:27)

Does Jesus believe that all of His sheep can hear His voice?

How can He be so confident about this?

Then Pilate said to him, "So you are a king?" Jesus answered, "You say that I am a king. For this purpose I was born and for this purpose I have come into the world—to bear witness to the truth. Everyone who is of the truth listens to my voice." (Joh 18:37)

How does this verse give us guidance about what can hinder our ability to hear God's voice clearly?

Let me ask you only this: Did you receive the Spirit by works of the law or by hearing of faith? … Does he who supplies the Spirit to you and works miracles among you do so by works of the law, or by hearing of faith—
(Gal 3:2-5)

What is the relationship between hearing God, faith, and the operation of the Holy Spirit in our lives?

SECTION 2- RECOGNIZING GOD SPEAK SPEAKING

Read the Scriptures below.

a. UNDERLINE every phrase that indicates a characteristic of God speaking

b. ANSWER the questions following each of the verses below based on the verse immediately above the question.

I write to you, fathers, because you know him who is from the beginning. I write to you, young men, because you are strong, and the word of God abides in you, and you have overcome the evil one. (1Jn 2:14)

Select the best answer. According to this verse, we hear God:
  a) Only on rare occasions when you need special guidance
  b) Mainly by intruding thoughts in our mind
  c) Mainly by dreams, visions, and impressions
  d) God's word lives in us as a continual awareness

I press on toward the goal for the prize of the upward call of God in Christ Jesus. Let those of us who are mature think this way, and if in anything you think otherwise, God will reveal that also to you. (Php 3:14-15)

Have you ever gotten off track spiritually? According to these verses, how did you know?

Long ago, at many times and in many ways, God spoke to our fathers by the prophets, but in these last days he has spoken to us by his Son, whom he appointed the heir of all things, through whom also he created the world. (Heb. 1:1-2)

But that is not the way you learned Christ!—assuming that you have heard about him and were taught in him, as the truth is in Jesus, to put off your old self, which belongs to your former manner of life and is corrupt through deceitful desires, and to be renewed in the spirit of your minds, and to put on the new self, created after the likeness of God in true righteousness and holiness. (Eph 4:20-24)

According to the verses above, what is the relationship between God speaking, Jesus Christ, and walking in your identity in Christ?

But the Helper, the Holy Spirit, whom the Father will send in my name, he will teach you all things and bring to your remembrance all that I have said to you. (John 14:26)

How does the Holy Spirit use our memory to speak to us?

REFLECTION

Can you remember a time in which God used your memory to speak to you?

SECTION 3- VARIOUS MODES OF GOD SPEAK SPEAKING

Read the Scriptures below.

a. UNDERLINE every phrase that indicates one of the ways in which God can speak

b. ANSWER the questions following each of the verses below based on the verse immediately above the question.

"

'And in the last days it shall be, God declares, that I will pour out my Spirit on all flesh, and your sons and your daughters shall prophesy, and your young men shall see visions, and your old men shall dream dreams; even on my male servants and female servants in those days I will pour out my Spirit, and they shall prophesy. (Act 2:17-18)

For to one is given through the Spirit the utterance of wisdom, and to another the utterance of knowledge according to the same Spirit, to another faith by the same Spirit, to another gifts of healing by the one Spirit, to another the working of miracles, to another prophecy, to another the ability to distinguish between spirits, to another various kinds of tongues, to another the interpretation of tongues. (1Co 12:8-10)

From the verses in this section above, list the ways in which God can speak through His people.

From the list of the ways in which God can speak *through His people*, what does that show us about the ways in which God speaks *to His people?*

All Scripture is breathed out by God and profitable for teaching, for reproof, for correction, and for training in righteousness, that the man of God may be complete, equipped for every good work. (2Ti 3:16-17)

For the word of God is living and active, sharper than any two-edged sword, piercing to the division of soul and of spirit, of joints and of marrow, and discerning the thoughts and intentions of the heart. (Heb 4:12)

According to the previous verses, answer True or False:

_____ When we read the Bible, God is speaking directly to us.

_____ God's written Word is always living and active.

_____ When we receive God's written Word by faith, we are hearing God.

SECTION 4- GOD'S CHARACTER AND GOD'S VOICE

Read the Scriptures below.

a. UNDERLINE every phrase that indicates one of the characteristics of God speaking

b. ANSWER the questions following each of the verses below based on the verse immediately above the question.

(I write)…that their hearts may be encouraged, being knit together in love, to reach all the riches of full assurance of understanding and the knowledge of God's mystery, which is Christ, in whom are hidden all the treasures of wisdom and knowledge. (Col 2:2-3)

Based on the verses above, answer True or False:

_____ If I'm hearing thoughts that sound true that discourage me and give me a sense of hopelessness, it may still be God.

_____ When God speaks, He encourages our hearts to empower love.

_____ To hear God, we must be willing to face our fears and listen to courage.

_____ To hear God, we must be willing to face the attitudes and mindsets the keep us from loving like Christ.

_____ Knowing Jesus Christ is blasé. Hearing God in a fresh "now word" is where the excitement is.

On the other hand, the one who prophesies speaks to people for their upbuilding and encouragement and consolation. The one who speaks in a tongue builds up himself, but the one who prophesies builds up the church. (1Co 14:3-4)

If, when God speaks through His people He speaks for their "upbuilding, encouragement, and consolation," what does this show us about how to recognize God speaking to us?

For those who live according to the flesh set their minds on the things of the flesh, but those who live according to the Spirit set their minds on the things of the Spirit. For to set the mind on the flesh is death, but to set the mind on the Spirit is life and peace. (Rom 8:5-6)

From the verses above, fill out the chart below:

Fleshly Mind	Mind of the Spirit

III. LOOK OUT
PRACTICE

Recognizing the difference between carnal mindsets and the mind of Christ is the key to hearing God clearly.

- **The carnal mind is set on earthly things, not the things of God.** The old man is driven by "my rights" "my stuff" "my advancement" "me, myself, and mine", whereas the Spirit of God empowers you to "set your mind on things above", to "seek first the Kingdom of God", to "deny yourself, take up your cross daily, and follow Jesus".

- **There is no spiritual power in the carnal mind.** The mind of the old man brings a lack of spiritual power, vitality, and reality and brings death by advancing a "way that seems right to a man" (Prov. 14:12)

- **The carnal mind contradicts faith and a lifestyle of redeeming love.** "Faith pleases God" but the carnal mind cannot please God. It refuses to love sacrificially and does not take risks for the sake of the Kingdom of God.

For the following statements, characterize them as "C" (carnal) or "S" (Spirit). Then identify and discuss the determining phrases and words.

When someone didn't get healed instantly...

_____ "what's wrong with me. Why isn't God doing anything?"

_____ "don't worry. This has to go. Jesus is Lord!"

When you see an opportunity to speak to a stranger and show them God's love...

_____ "I know I should talk to them, but they are going to think I'm a freak."

_____ "they might think I'm a freak, but I'm going to talk with them anyway."

When someone brushes you off and gives you the cold shoulder...

_____ "after the way they've treated me, they better not expect any favors from me."

_____ "after what Jesus has done for me, it doesn't even phase me. I'm just going to keep on loving them!"

When finances run low and bills run high...

_____ "Of course I'm worried. Who wouldn't be?"

_____ "Okay God. I don't know how you're going to do it, but I know you will."

When the sermon topic is "win the world for Jesus"...

_____ "I've been faithfully attending and supporting this church, living a decent life, raising my family, and giving what I can. I think that's I'm doing about all God expects out of me. I'm not a pastor for crying out loud."

_____ "Lord, once again I offer my whole life as worship, to grow up into Christ, and to make disciples who walk in His fullness. Just give me clarity about the next step to take now!"

PLAN

Jesus us commands each one of us to "Go and make disciples!" God can use you to help others walk in His fullness.

This workbook is a powerful tool that you can use. You don't have to know everything or be a great communicator. You only need to be willing to invest some time in helping someone else. One of the best ways to truly learn anything is to teach it to someone else. This tool makes it easy to do.

Who do you know that might be interested in going this workbook with you? Brainstorm ALL the possibilities. Don't evaluate too much. Make a list:

Now, prayerfully review the list and circle the highest priority candidates.

How to ask. You can say something like, "Would you be interested in getting together somewhere convenient for you and learning from the Bible about how we can experience God in our daily lives?" Then set your first appointment.

Get started this week!

APPENDIX 1
SUGGESTIONS FOR *YOUR PLACE IN THE SON* GROUP LEADERS

1) **Multiply NEW GROUPS** - Here's how— Encourage each person in your group to begin to share with other people about the things that God is doing in their lives. As they find people who are interested and eager to grow, they should NOT invite them to join this group. Your group can receive visitors, but I'd encourage, that instead of growing your own group, challenge everyone in your group to begin to work through this same material with their friends and start new groups! You can help them.

2) **Break the "Bible Study" Mold by doing the Word together-** Your biggest job is to help people do what they dream of doing by:
   - providing a supportive, encouraging, and focused environment
   - celebrate people taking risks and overcoming their fears. Results will follow.
   - do your assignments with people, especially the ones who need more support.
   - keep everyone focused on Jesus and allowing Him to be Himself in us

3) **Facilitate the meetings by being a Leader, a Coach, and a Learner.** Use the manual as a tool to bring focus to the group discussion. Don't be the teacher or preacher. If you make your living room a mini-pulpit, your couch will become a comfy pew. These meetings are intended to draw out participation, involvement, and interaction.

4) **Use the Training Manual as the playing field.** When the "ball rolls out of bounds", refer to the manual to get things back on track. How? Usually a smile, a little chuckle, and an "Okay, now where were we? Let's get back on track gang" will do the trick.

5) **During "Look Back":**
   - Start with a good example so people have an idea about how to share.
   - If anyone is talking too much, just say, "This is good, but we need to wrap this up to allow time for others. 1 more minute."

6) Involve everyone during the LESSON by going around the room to take turns reading, calling out underlined phrases, circled phrases, answer to questions, etc.

7) Many chapters will require more than one session (unless your group does part of the lessons as "homework"- see #11 for more about this), but be sure to divide every meeting evenly into three sections—"Look Back" "Lesson" and "Look Out"— so that every meeting contains encouragement and sharing, Bible learning, and practical hands-on ministry with goal setting for practical steps of faith.

8) Keep the focus on Jesus Christ and advancing His Kingdom because of His redeeming love. People are very prone towards falling into a "performance" mindset— basing their joy, security, and worth in their own ability to perform. Your main role is to help everyone keep their eyes on Jesus Christ. He's the only performer in the group! People are also very conditioned to maintain the status quo. The life of Jesus Christ must become our new normal, so we must declare war on the comfort zones of the flesh. It's not about us. It's about Jesus Christ and His love for others. Lead the way by example!

9) Take advantage of the additional resources to prepare yourself and encourage the group. I would highly recommend that you read the chapter of the book, *Your Place in the Son,* that corresponds with each lesson. All these additional resources are available at FullSpeedImpact.com.

10) Multiply leaders for the group by selecting at least one or two apprentices from DAY 1. Give them additional responsibility, opportunities, and support. If you only have one or two people in your group, you should consider them both apprentices and give them opportunities to lead the group sessions while you are together so they develop their own leadership skills in a supportive environment.

11) Some groups may choose to complete the lesson as homework, and come together mainly to discuss highlights and work on the practice exercises. This is a great way to keep the group focused on being "doers of the Word" not merely a "Bible study". If you take this approach, I suggest that rather than going over each verse one by one, pull out the highlights by asking review/over questions to facilitate a discussion the "Lesson".

If you chose to do the lessons as "homework" then review them together, this may allow you to spend more time focusing on the activation exercises. In that case, here are some simple overview/review questions that can be used to facilitate the discussion:

1. What are the main truths that you understood?

2. What encouraged or challenged you the most from what you read this week?

3. What practical difference does God want these truths to make in the way we live?

ADDITIONAL RESOURCES FROM THE AUTHOR

You will find additional resources from Andy Hayner at his ministry website **FullSpeedImpact.com**.

If you want to learn how to experience the power of your identity in Christ, *Your Place in the Son* is the book for you. You will see the reality of your union with Jesus Christ like never before and learn how to break free from negative emotions and carnal mindsets to walk in the freedom, joy, and power of the Spirit of God. Reading this book will absolutely transform your walk with God and show you how to walk in the victory and love of Jesus Christ.

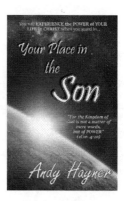

Jesus Christ died to give you the authority and power to heal the sick. **Born to Heal** will show you how to walk in the power and love of Jesus Christ and heal the sick as a lifestyle. Never again will you feel helpless in the face of sickness and pain. This book is packed with Biblical and practical training that will revolutionize your life!

The *Born to Heal Interactive Training Manual* is a powerful tool to learn the life-changing content of *Born to Heal* in small groups through direct interaction with the Scriptures. This is perfect to use even for those who have not read Born to Heal, or can be used for those who want to supplement and reinforce what they read in Born to Heal. It's designed with LifeTeams, small groups, and discipleship relationships in mind. You'll **learn for yourself** *through interactive, inductive Bible studies and life-changing practical activation exercises.* The perfect resourcc for raising up supernatural disciples of Jesus Christ!

 **God Heals Birth Defects— First Fruits** is a revolutionary book that will encourage, challenge, and equip you to minister healing in seemingly impossible situations. Written with a team of amazing parents from around the world, this book is packed with testimonies from parents who are seeing God heal their children who are afflicted with diagnosis such as autism, down syndrome, and cerebral palsy. If you are looking for hope and practical Biblical answers that will empower you to minister healing to those afflicted with birth defects, and are ready to step into a lifestyle that truly manifests "All things are possible with God," this book is for you!

Spirit Cry, is a powerful devotional tool that will accelerate your personal mind renewal and revolutionize your personal experience of God by adding incredible depth, insight, and power to your personal fellowship with God. You will learn how to use the Scriptures to speak to the Father as a son and to hear the Father speak to you as a son. Get this and unleash your Spirit Cry!

The book, *Immersed into God*, is comprehensive equipping to mobilize you to walk in the fullness of Jesus Christ and impact the world around you! Filled with examples, Biblical insights, and practical coaching, you will learn to experience God's power in your own life and to release His power to others by healing the sick, prophetic evangelism, and

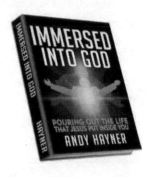

establishing disciples of Jesus Christ who walk in His supernatural power.

The *Immersed into God Interactive Training Manual* is a powerful tool to learn the life-changing content of *Immersed into God* in small groups, LifeTeams, and personal discipleship relationships. You'll **learn for yourself** *through interactive, inductive Bible studies and life-changing practical activation exercises.* This is the perfect resource for raising up supernatural disciples of Jesus Christ!

ABOUT THE AUTHOR

Andy Hayner mobilizes believers to walk in the fullness of Jesus Christ world-wide. He is recognized for having a gift to impart a profound revelation of the believer's union with Jesus Christ in a simple, understandable way that unleashes greater depths of the love and power of God. He has a passion for hands-on disciple making that has been developed through over twenty years of Christian service as a missionary, a pastor, and a church planter. He is the founder of Full Speed Impact Ministries and volunteers as a Regional Director for John G. Lake Ministries, the oldest and most successful healing ministry in existence today. He holds a Masters of Divinity from Columbia International University Graduate School of Missions. He resides in Wisconsin with his wife and three children.

A missionary at heart, Andy travels widely to ministers to churches, small groups, conferences, and individuals wherever God opens the door. Although he travels widely, he endeavors to establish ongoing relationships with churches to be a regular outside resource for the sake of the Kingdom. To enquire about having Andy minister in your area, please contact Andy directly at FullSpeedAndy@gmail.com.